SKIING

STEP BY STEP TO SUCCESS

ROB REICHENFELD
with
ANNA MARIE BRUECHERT

The Crowood Press

First published in 1992 by
The Crowood Press Ltd
Ramsbury, Marlborough
Wiltshire SN8 2HR

© The Crowood Press Ltd 1992

British Library Cataloguing in Publication Data

A catalogue record for this book is available from the British Library.

ISBN 1 85223 707 4

Picture credits

All photographs for this book were taken by Rob Reichenfeld in Verbier, Switzerland. Many thanks to M. Moix and TELE VERBIER, for their full co-operation.

Acknowledgements

I would like to thank the dedicated professionals whose expertise helped make this book a reality. The methodology used in the snowboarding, telemarking and racing chapters owes much to the knowledge of the following people: Matt Gilder who generously gave his time to demonstrate and explain snowboarding methods. Matt is a snowboard examiner for APSI and teaches snowboarding for the Thredbo, Australia, ski school. Steven Lee who demonstrated and explained the latest World Cup ski racing techniques. Stevie has represented Australia in World Cup competition for the last ten years. Peter Mack, a champion telemark skier from Australia, who explained the method for teaching telemark skiing. Peter has since written a manual for Australian telemark skiing teachers.

Thanks are also due to the models: Anna Marie Bruechert, Matt Gilder, Steven Lee, Rolf Liechti, Lisa Nicholas, Hans Solmssen, Kusan Staubli and Kiki Thompson. Rolf Liechti is a ski instructor from Queenstown, New Zealand; Lisa Nicholas is a professional skier and former Australian Freestyle Ski Team member and World Cup mogul competitor; Kusan Staubli is a Tibetan-born Swiss skier and former top junior racer. He presently teaches skiing in Gstaad and demonstrates techniques for Swiss ski-teacher examinations; Hans Solmssen, born and raised in Hawaii, is an apprentice alpine guide in Verbier, Switzerland and demonstrated telemark technique.

I should also like to recognize the companies who were kind enough to sponsor us with the latest gear – all of it excellent and highly recommended: Asolo telemark boots; Emery snowboard bindings; Hooger Booger snowboards; Marker alpine ski bindings; Poilloux/ Vuarnet sunglasses; Rossignol alpine skis, snowboards and snowboard boots; Rottefella telemark bindings; Schneider ski clothing; Scott goggles and ski poles; Scarpa telemark boots; Tecnica alpine ski boots; Wombat bindings.

Finally, a word of thanks to my many skiing buddies who have provided inspiration in both skiing and photography over the years. A few among the many: Trevor Avedissian, Gary Bigham, John Falkiner, Ace Kvale, Craig Hesse, Henrik Oscarsson, Glen Plake, Mike Powers, Mary Jo Tiampo-Oscarsson, and my first ski teacher, my father.

Typeset by Acūté, Stroud, Gloucestershire.
Printed in Malaysia

Contents

THE SKIER'S CODE

International Code of Practice
for Skiers

Here are a few basic rules of the road put together by the Fédération Internationale de Ski (published March/May 1990). Everybody should know these before venturing onto the slopes.

Rule 1   Respect for others
A skier must behave in such a way that he does not endanger or prejudice others. Ski slowly on beginners' slopes and don't pass close to slow skiers.

Rule 2   Control of speed and skiing
A skier must ski in control.He must adapt his speed and manner of skiing to his personal ability and to the prevailing conditions of terrain, snow and weather as well as to the density of traffic.

Rule 3   Choice of route
A skier coming from behind must choose his route in such a way that he does not endanger skiers ahead.

Rule 4   Overtaking
A skier may overtake another skier above or below and to the right or to the left, provided that he leaves enough space for the overtaken skier to make any voluntary or involuntary movement.

Rule 5   Entering and starting
A skier entering a marked run or starting again after stopping must look up and down the run to make sure that he can do so without endangering himself or others.

Rule 6   Stopping on the piste
Unless absolutely necessary, a skier must avoid stopping on the piste in narrow places or where visibility is restricted. After a fall in such a place, a skier must move clear of the piste as soon as possible.

Rule 7   Climbing and descending on foot
Both a skier climbing or descending on foot must keep to the sides of the piste.

Rule 8   Respect for signs and markings
A skier must respect all signs and markings.

Rule 9   Assistance
At accidents, every skier is bound to assist. Place skis in a cross; keep victim warm; send for help.

Rule 10   Identification
Every skier and witness, whether a responsible party or not, must exchange names and addresses following an accident.

Following are a few more pieces of advice.

1. Don't jump in areas where you cannot see the landing first; there may be skiers standing below.
2. Note what time the lifts close – you don't want to be stuck for the night on the wrong side of the mountain.
3. Protect nature – don't harm trees or shrubs with your skis.
4. Rest when you are tired.

Introduction

Skiing: Step by Step to Success has been written and photographed as a straightforward and comprehensive guide to ski technique. Whether you are a complete novice or ski at a more advanced level, this book is designed to develop your skills in a progression of easy, confidence-building stages.

The following points are central to the book's effectiveness and have been outlined to help you make the most of time spent both with this book and on the slopes.

Skiing is not a series of static positions but continuous movement within a sphere of motion. The sequence photography throughout the book brings this movement to life and illustrates that no one position is an end in itself. Use the photo-

sequences to imagine yourself as the skier, sensing the skier's motion as if it were your own. This process, called visualization, is an effective method of discovering the key to new moves.

Pay special attention to the terrain guidelines throughout the text. Using the correct terrain is an essential element for smooth progress and often neglected by beginning skiers. Advancing to steeper slopes before learning the necessary skills is tempting, but can lead to bad habits detrimental to long-term progress. Follow the terrain guidelines carefully to prevent later frustration. Remember, it is easier to build on good habits than correct bad ones!

Books, magazines and instructional videos are all valuable aids to

learning and improving technique, but none can fully replace the hands-on attention of a professional instructor. While you may not wish to spend your entire vacation in class, lessons can provide a solid foundation on which to build. This book reinforces lessons at every level and explains the principles behind them.

Snowboarding and telemarking are two exciting skiing variations with an ever-increasing international following. Chapters on each have been included for those of you keen to expand your skiing horizons.

Snowboarding is a relatively new way to have fun on the slopes. The simplicity behind both the technique and equipment, coupled with the appeal of free-flowing movement, makes snowboarding a highly pleasurable and worthwhile endeavour.

Telemarking is an old ski technique enjoying a modern revival. Recent technical advances in equipment have made telemarking an effective skiing method both on and off piste and brought this graceful technique back on to the slopes and into popularity. Both snowboarding and telemarking are presented in comprehensive chapters progressing from the beginner's first day, to advanced techniques, including a full introduction to the equipment.

Whether alpine skiing, telemarking or snowboarding, don't forget the most important goal of all: Have fun!

Kusan Staubli

1 Alpine Ski Equipment

Good ski gear is an investment. Quality equipment makes skiing easier and more fun. However, top-of-the-line gear is always expensive and often not necessary for the beginner. The most expensive models are designed for experts and have many features that the beginner would be unlikely to make use of.

When you are first learning to ski, I recommend that you rent, rather than buy, equipment. This lets you try the sport and sample various types of gear before buying. If you plan on skiing one or two weeks a year, renting skis makes sense. Ski rental is not only convenient, it also allows you to upgrade skis as technique and ability improve. Once committed to the sport you should buy your own boots, as rental boots are hard to adapt to.

Most resorts have ski shops providing the latest-model skis and boots. Buying or renting, deal only with professional ski shops, whose staff are well trained.

BOOTS

Well-fitting boots are most important. Painful, cold feet are a misery best avoided. Good ski boots provide not only comfort, but also control. They are the link between you and the snow. Begin by renting, rather than buying boots until you have more experience.

It can be uncomfortable adapting to different boots and your own can be custom fitted, ensuring better fit and ski feel. It is rare that borrowing boots is a good idea; the same shoe size does not necessarily mean the same boot size.

Buy boots only in a speciality ski shop, one that guarantees the fit.

Fig 1   A Rossignol ski tip, circa 1945. Wood laminate, coloured base, screw-on metal edges, metal tip protector.

Fig 2   A Rossignol ski tip, circa 1992. Fibreglass composite construction, sintered plastic base, steel edges, anti-vibration system, plastic tip.

This same shop will charge to adjust boots bought elsewhere. Buying boots at a ski resort makes sense. Problems are easier to take care of if the technician can see fresh pressure or stress marks on your feet. If your boots give you serious or even occasional pain, stop skiing and have them adjusted immediately. Should you badly bruise an ankle bone, recuperation can take weeks.

The price of boots usually goes up according to the standard of skier the boot is designed for. Boots with many fitting features cost more than simpler models.

Sizing

Boot manufacturers are still working on a standard sizing system. Use the numbers only as a guide. The most common sizing error is to settle on boots that are too large. In the correct size, toes should be almost touching the end when you are standing up straight. They'll move back when you flex your ankles. Beware of being sold too large a boot just because it feels good.

An easy method for checking boot size is as follows: Remove the inner liner. Put the boot on, slide your toes to the front and check that there is a gap of approximately one finger's thickness behind your heel. This will ensure sufficient but not excessive room for the liner. Checking boot size this way is more precise than just trying on the boot without removing the liner. It takes some time for the inner liner to shape to your feet and you could otherwise be fooled into buying boots that are too large.

Once you have found a shell of the right length, replace the liner, put the boot on again and check that your heel is held snugly in place. When you arch your foot the heel may lift slightly, but should stay put when you are flexing forwards.

Assuming the boot matches your foot type (wide, narrow, etc.), if the boot shell is the right length, it should be possible to make the boot fit by adapting the liners to your feet. Foam-filled liners exist for special problems, and are popular with racers demanding a precise fit. These liners are supplied with some high-performance boots or can be bought separately.

Flex

Smooth flex is important. Beware of boots that bend easily as you begin to flex your ankle, then stiffen suddenly. These will surely bruise shins. Pressure against the shin must increase gradually as you flex forwards.

Entry-level boots flex forwards easily. Boots designed for advanced skiers are stiffer, and unsuitable for beginners or intermediate skiers. The reason for this is that stiff boots are needed at high speeds, but are otherwise a hindrance. At the top level of the sport, skiers fine tune the flex of their boots very carefully. If you had the chance to look closely at a World Cup racer's boots, you might see all manner of customizing, rivets, steel plates and the like.

Entry Systems

In the good old days, laces were the principal means of closing boots. Now we have entry systems: front, mid or rear entry (the part of the boot that opens to let your foot in).

Rear-entry boots are favoured by rental shops. They are easy to fit: adjustments are made with internally moving pads and straps that fill up the gaps and snug your foot

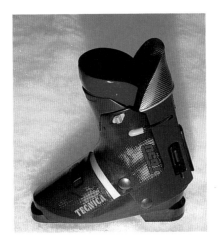

Fig 3   A Tecnica rear-entry boot.

Fig 4   An overlap-entry boot.

into the shell. Front-entry, or overlapping, shells, are adjusted by tightening buckles on the outside of the boot, and may have some internal adjusters too. In general this system provides the most precise fit, for good ski 'feel', and is favoured by ski racers and advanced skiers. Mid-entry boots combine features found in both types.

Stiffer boots are favoured by advanced skiers. Softer versions are recommended for intermediate skiers.

Footbeds

Custom footbeds are insoles shaped to the bottoms of your feet. They are a necessity for advanced skiers and all skiers with problem feet, but they are also a good investment for intermediate and beginning skiers.

As we control skis through the bottoms of our feet, fit in this sensitive area is very important.

SKIS

Skis are made to match every type of skier, from the first-timer who moves very slowly, to the speed

skier flying down at over 200kph (125mph). Beginners will find soft-flexing, light skis easiest to use. These should be just under head height in length. After your first few endeavours, change to skis about head height.

Your correct length depends on size, ability and the type of skiing that you do. The key factor is how fast you ski. Longer skis are more

Fig 5   Modern ski equipment.

HOW TO SHOP FOR A SKI BOOT

1. Buy boots only from shops with trained and qualified boot-fitting technicians. Make sure that they guarantee the fit.

2. Pick a time when neither you, nor the shop staff, are in a hurry. Expect to spend one to two hours in the shop. It takes this long to fit boots and to feel pressure points.

3. Establish your skiing ability and price range. Advanced skiers will need to spend more.

4. Are your feet extra wide or narrow? Let the salesperson know. Not all brands fit all feet.

5. To find out your size, do a shell fit. Take the liner out and put your foot in, with toes to the front. Check that there is room for one finger behind the heel. If there is room for two fingers, try the shell that is the next size smaller. To be certain, I usually find the size that is definitely too small and take the next one up. (Shell sizes usually go up in whole, not half, sizes. In most brands, thicker liners and toe caps take care of half sizes.)

6. If length is OK, check the volume. Close buckles, straps, screws, etc. Adjust until the boot feels comfortable, and snug all over. If any closure needs to be adjusted to the maximum, check that shorter cables or bales are available, as boots become slightly bigger with use.

7. Stay in the boots for at least half an hour before purchasing. Have a walk around, flex your ankles. Is the flex smooth? Are you in any pain? Use the time to check out skis and clothes, or talk to the technician. This time is necessary to highlight problem areas. Have the technician explain the boots' features and how they adjust.

8. After taking the boots home, and before going skiing, spend some hours in them. Watch TV, walk around; remember you'll be spending all day in them on the mountain. If they don't feel good at home – and providing you haven't skied in them – it's not too late to change them.

stable, shorter skis turn more quickly. Most men end up skiing on skis between 200cm and 205cm (79in and 81in) and women on skis between 190cm and 195cm (75in and 77in); intermediate skiers can subtract about 5cm (2in) from this range.

Ski manufacturers have come up with three categories of skis to match these target groups. A code letter, usually in the binding area, marks which group a ski belongs to. The letters are as follows: L for beginners and very slow skiers; A for intermediates, able to negotiate moderate slopes, at medium speed; S for advanced, faster skiers.

In general, avoid bargain-basement, supermarket skis and stick to well-known brands. Trained ski-shop personnel should be able to help you select a model and size to suit. While it is possible to give general advice about ski length, flex also determines what size would be most suitable. This is hard for the non-expert to judge, so ask for advice about any particular ski that interests you. Remember that heavier people, of every standard require stiffer skis than lighter people do. As I said before, it is best to rent a similar model before buying. Ski shops normally deduct a day's rental charge from the price should you decide to buy.

For advanced skiers, where you ski also affects the type and size of ski that you need. If your preference is for high-speed, long radius turns on smoothly groomed slopes, a long, giant-slalom-type ski will suit you best. Those who prefer shorter turns or moguls, and often ski icy slopes, will find a slalom-type ski most agreeable.

If you already own skis, and they have been in storage over the summer, they should be checked before being used. Ensure that the running surface is clean, free of holes and waxed to ensure that the skis slide easily over the snow. The edges should be rust-free, without major damage or burrs. Well-maintained skis are important for safety and control.

BINDINGS

Modern ski bindings provide a high degree of security. Like any safety equipment, they will only perform as designed if they are properly adjusted and maintained. For this reason, make sure that a qualified technician gives your bindings an annual check-up. If the technician refuses to service your bindings because they are of an older design, take note: he has your best interests at heart. Following his advice could save you unnecessary injury. Out-of-date bindings must be replaced.

When servicing or installing new bindings, the technician should ask about your weight and ability. These factors also determine which model of binding you should have. Each manufacturer designs bindings for every standard; these vary in features and spring weights. Be honest with the salesperson, and you won't go far wrong. A reputable shop will not let a customer out of the door with anything unsuitable. Before leaving, make sure that you are shown how to use the bindings!

POLES

Ski poles are a very simple but necessary piece of equipment. Budget and ability can be your guide. The most expensive poles are well balanced and light, with special models available for racing and ski touring. Beginning skiers can settle for cheaper models, as these are usually easier to bend back should you fall on them. If you lose a pole basket (the ring at the bottom), have it replaced immediately. Some poles have releasable straps, a good safety feature. When buying poles, make sure that the grip feels comfortable in your hand.

Fig 6   An old ski binding, designed to hold the ski on the foot but not to release in case of a fall – old wooden skis usually broke before the skier's leg did.

Fig 7   Modern bindings release in every possible direction and have contributed greatly to skiers' safety. These are Marker bindings.

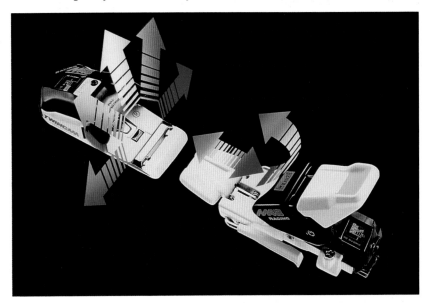

Pole Length

The correct length for ski poles is a matter of personal taste. The following rule of thumb will suit most people. Turn the pole upside down and grip it just above the basket, resting the handle on the ground. The pole is the correct length when your forearm is parallel to the

Fig 8   The pole is the correct length when the forearm is parallel to the ground.

ground (when wearing ski boots). Racers often use quite long poles to aid them in getting a quick start, and mogul skiers use very short ones.

CLOTHING

Beginners especially require comfortable, well-fitting and warm gear, designed for activity in the snow. When first learning to ski you will walk more than later on, fall down more and stand around more. It's a lot more fun to be warm and dry than cold and wet.

Hats are very important; remember that we lose a lot of heat through our heads. Always take a hat if you are skiing at high altitude – weather can quickly change. In warmer weather a headband is a good accessory.

While your clothing must keep you warm, overheating can be a problem. Avoid thick, down clothing designed for winter activities for which freedom of movement is not as critical as for skiing.

A practical method of dressing for the outdoors is to dress in layers: wicking underwear, a ski turtleneck with zip neck, a fleece or wool sweater, a windproof/water-resistant jacket and bib pants. Dressing in many thin layers makes it much easier to control your temperature than wearing one thick layer.

Modern technology has provided some truly amazing fabrics, used to manufacture clothing for any weather condition. Some are practically waterproof, yet 'breathe' allowing moisture from perspiration to escape (Gore-Tex is a good example). Other fabrics (worn next to the skin) wick moisture to the outer layers. Synthetics work better than cotton or wool for this, though I don't recommend older versions of polypropylene (it starts to smell with age); capilene, for example, is better.

One-piece ski suits are a warm, comfortable alternative, especially for skiing in deep powder snow. They can be awkward in restaurants or on days when temperatures rise.

Unfortunately these specialized garments are expensive. If fashion is not your prime reason for buying a new suit, take advantage of the great deals that can be found in the summer, when ski shops clear out last year's stock to make room for the coming season's colours. Planning ahead can pay dividends: quality for a good price – rare enough these days.

Don't wear jeans or cotton trousers. These soak up moisture, which then freezes – most uncomfortable. Use quality water-resistant gear, with snug-fitting cuffs, well-sealed pockets and high close-fitting collar with zipper flap.

Ski Socks

Good ski socks are important. Wear one pair, preferably specially designed for use in ski boots. Some racers use a thin stocking for improved ski feel, but almost everybody else is better off in a proper ski sock. Wool and cotton are suitable if they are of a smooth design. Some modern materials, such as capilene, are even better at wicking moisture away and keeping feet dry. Avoid socks with a raised pattern or ribs, which can cause discomfort.

Sunglasses

High-quality sunglasses are essential. Use only glasses that are designed to cope with strong radiation, and are capable of filtering out 100 per cent of UV B rays (the most dangerous kind). Snow is an extremely reflective surface, and the light is genuinely dangerous to your eyes. On no account should glasses designed for cosmetic or city pur-

Fig 9   Quality sunglasses filter 100 per cent UV B. Don't skimp on this vital purchase.

poses be used. These can cause more harm than good – the dark tint makes your irises open up and un-filtered UV B rays stream in, possibly causing serious damage to your eyes. Don't skimp on this vital purchase.

Goggles

Skiing during a storm is fun, but not without good goggles. Goggles for bad weather have specially tinted lenses to increase contrast. Yellowish-orange tints are popular, but look through a few different models to find your personal preference. After selecting lens colour, the next choice is between one lens or two, or even models with built-in fans! The object of all this technology is to prevent the lens from fogging. There is a big differential in temperature between your face and the air; perspiration adds to the problem.

Fig 10   Goggles protect your eyes from snowflakes and improve contrast in poor visibility.

Lisa visualizes her line.

While the manufacturers tell us otherwise, almost any goggles will fog at some stage. Don't forget to take along a soft cotton cloth to dry them out (a specially treated cloth is required for coated lenses).

A trick that I have found handy during heavy snowstorms is to ride only outdoor lifts, such as chairlifts and T bars. This keeps me cool (skiing deep snow is warm work), and the problem of goggles instantly fogging on getting into a crowded cable car is avoided. (Make sure that you wear weatherproof clothing.)

Sunscreen

In these days of decreased ozone and increased risk of skin cancer, sunscreen is especially important. Protect all exposed flesh with a high-factor (at least 15) sunscreen (not tanning lotion). The sun is much stronger at high altitudes than at low ones, and snow increases radiation. Ear lobes and under the tip of nose are often forgotten, even though they are especially sensitive and vulnerable. Rays reflected up-

Rolf Liechti.

EQUIPMENT CHECKLIST

Skis (with bindings).
Boots.
Poles.
Weatherproof clothing. In midwinter, one-piece suits are practical; for spring, ski pants worn with a sweater and windbreaker are more versatile.
Good-quality ski gloves. (Thick mittens are warmer in extreme cold.)
A warm wool or fleece hat (even on sunny days it can be cold up the mountain or in the shade).
Sunscreen – at least factor 15 (not tanning lotion).
Lip balm – protects your lips from sun and wind.
High-quality dark glasses designed for use at high altitude.
Goggles (in case the weather changes).
Lightweight windbreaker. Especially useful in springtime should clouds roll in.
Ski-lift pass.
Piste and lift map.
Be prepared and nothing will stop you from having fun.

ACCESSORIES

The checklist covered most of the equipment that skiers need, but there are a few items that you may wish to consider in addition.

For extreme cold and wind:

Hat with ear flaps.
Face mask (neoprene, silk, leather, wool and fleece all have their advocates).
Neck gaiter (big, roll-up collar worn round the neck).
Insulated boot covers, which help to keep feet toasty.

Boot and ski bags to protect your equipment when travelling.
Possibly a small backpack or fanny pack.
Wet stone to touch up ski edges on the hill, and edge sharpener and waxing kit to maintain skis.

In deep powder snow:

Avalanche beeper – get one and learn how to use it perfectly.
Lightweight shovel – for digging snow pits and avalanche rescue.
Long, fluorescent powder cords to make skis easier to locate.
One-piece ski suits with zipped pockets and tight-fitting wrists, ankles and neck.

wards from the snow make these areas prone to painful burns. Bad sunburn calls for a day or two spent indoors – not a popular way to spend vacation time.

Reapply sunscreen periodically through the day, especially in springtime.

Gloves

Modern gloves have taken full advantage of the latest in technology. Good gloves are expensive but they are worth the money. Gore-Tex liners are common, and Thinsulate and other lightweight insulators are popular. Look for hard-wearing quality in stitching and zips: good gloves should last. Removable liners make gloves easier to dry out over your lunch break, which is a distinct advantage as wet hands get cold very quickly.

For extreme cold, mittens are warmer than gloves. Having your fingers in contact with each other allows them to share the warmth.

2 Basics

Fig 11   For walking long distances, balance skis on your shoulder. Place them between the tip (front of ski) and binding.

Fig 12   If you have trouble carrying skis on your shoulder, entwine the skis and poles and carry them like a suitcase.

CARRYING SKIS

Handling skis and poles takes some getting used to, and is bound to feel awkward at first. Ease comes with time and practice.

For walking long distances, first slide ski bases together so that the brakes interlock. Now balance the skis on your shoulder, between the ski tip (front of ski) and binding. Initially the weight and balance of skis feels cumbersome but your shoulder will adapt, and carrying your skis this way leaves a hand free to handle poles, hat, goggles, etc.

If you have trouble carrying skis on your shoulder, entwine skis and poles and carry them like a suitcase. However, be warned: this will immediately label you as a 'punter' – ski jargon for tourist!

THE FALL LINE

This term describes the imaginary line down a slope that a rolling ball would follow, i.e. the path of least resistance.

Ski teachers continually use the fall line as a reference point, and the term is used frequently throughout this book for the same purpose.

TERRAIN

The ideal terrain for a beginner to learn on is a large bowl-shaped area, where gently rising slopes meet in a smooth, level runout. Gentle slopes allow for a gradual ascent up the hill as skills and confidence progress.

Beginners' slopes are most frequently located at the bottom of a resort's skiing area. This differs from one resort to the next, and

Fig 13   The fall line is the imaginary line down a slope that a rolling ball would follow: the path of least resistance.

14

sometimes the best area is higher up on an alpine plateau or glacier, accessible by cable car.

The beginners' terrain is not always as obvious as it may seem – good reason to spend your first few days with a professional instructor. If you are on the right slope, the chances are there will be many others like yourself. It is important to establish space of your own and, if possible, to avoid mainstream traffic.

Fig 14   A large bowl-shaped area is ideal for first-timers.

Get out of the clouds – come ski!

THE WARM-UP

Warm muscles stretch, cold muscles tear. Taking a little time to warm muscles is a wise habit. Besides helping to prevent injury, warming up with skis on eases your body into the transition from pedestrian to skier with a ready frame of mind. Do the exercises before starting to walk on skis; they are a simple and effective means of becoming familiar with the weight and balance of skis and boots.

Walk to the practice area, carrying your skis. Choose a level space away from the skier traffic for your warm-up. Place the skis side by side on the snow. Use your poles for support and step into the bindings. Make sure that they latch properly. Relax, feel your weight evenly distributed on each foot and avoid leaning on your poles. Slide the skis back and forth in the snow for a moment, then try a few simple exercises.

Note Stretch gently to avoid strain. Stretch left and right equally.

Figs 15(a)–(i)   A few simple exercises:

Fig 15(a)   Balance on one ski and move the other's tip up and down and twist it from side to side.

Fig 15(b)   If you have good balance, lift a ski in front of you, resting the tail in the snow, and stretch towards your knee.

Fig 15(c)   To stretch further, touch the toe of the raised foot.

Fig 15(d)   A more difficult stretch is to balance a ski behind you on its tip and stretch the muscles on the top of your thigh. This is a good stretch but a little tricky at first, and should not be attempted by those who feel less steady on one foot.

Fig 15(e)   Move your skis apart and stretch the insides of your legs.

Fig 15(f)   Run in place to 'get loose'. This exercise is very popular with racers before the start.

Fig 15(g)   Stand as low as you can.

Fig 15(h)   Stand as tall as you can.

Fig 15(i)   Try jumping in place. Flex your ankles and knees and rise quickly, springing up off the snow.

Many more warm-up exercises are possible before skiing. Here are a few more to switch on your skiing muscles:

1. Roll your knees from side to side;
2. The 'Charleston' – move your legs from knock-kneed to bow-legged;
3. Lean forwards and backwards against your boots;
4. Twist from side to side, with hands on your hips;
5. Flex your ankles, by pressing your shins against the front of your boots;
6. Finally, stand with feet about shoulder width apart, relax and do a few circles of your head, shoulders and waist. Now you are ready to start moving on skis.

GRIPPING POLES

Holding your poles is simple, but there is a correct way. Slip your hand through the strap from below and clasp the grip over the strap. Holding poles this way provides the best support.

FALLING SAFELY

Don't be anxious: falling is part of skiing, especially at first. Beginners frequently sit unplanned in the snow! Practising falling builds up confidence. Practise in soft snow that is not too deep. To fall, slowly sit to the side. If you are crossing a slope, sitting on the uphill side greatly reduces your fall. Keep your legs together and close to your body. If falling while in motion, avoid digging your skis and knees into the slope; just come to a sliding stop on your side.

Getting up from a Fall

Don't take your skis off if you fall. Sit on your bottom, with the skis below you, both facing across the slope in the same direction. Swing the skis around if you have landed below them. Bring the skis up close under your bottom, or shuffle yourself down to the skis in preparation for standing. To stand up easily, transfer your body weight over your feet with a forward rolling motion. This can be done only if your legs are under your bottom.

If you have trouble standing, poles may be used to assist. Hold

Figs 16(a) and (b) Gripping poles.

Fig 16(a) Hold the strap away from the handle and slip your hand through the strap from below.

Fig 16(b) Clasp the grip over the strap and adjust the strap so that it fits snugly on the back of your hand.

both poles together diagonally in front of you. Place the hand nearer the hill just above the pole baskets (the rings at the bottom end of the poles), and your other hand on top of the grips. Put the tips in the snow on the uphill side and use both hands to push. Do not place all your weight on the poles. The forward rolling action and leg muscles, not your arms, do most of the work.

Figs 17(a) and (b) Getting up from a fall. Transfer your body weight over your feet with a forward rolling motion, thus raising yourself upwards to a standing position. This can be done only if your legs are under your bottom. On the flat slopes, simultaneously flatten your skis onto the snow as you roll forwards, rolling them from edges to bases.

Rolf Liechti.

Fig 18 To use poles to assist you, hold both poles together diagonally in front of you, one hand on top of the pole grips and the other near the baskets. Put the tips of the poles in the snow on the uphill side, and use both hands to help yourself up, while transferring your body weight over your feet with a forward rolling motion.

THE BASIC STANCE

Standing well on skis is the key to progress. The basic stance is the same 'ready' position as that of many sports. You are ready for action, but relaxed, with ankles and knees slightly bent, weight evenly distributed on both feet, and skis hip width apart.

Having completed the warm-up, you should find yourself in a good stance naturally.

WALKING

Choose a smooth, flat place to practise. Remember the basic stance position and keep it relaxed. Crossing a flat area should be easier and faster with skis than without skis on.

Try walking around in a large circle without using your poles. Starting with the skis hip width apart, slide one ski forwards at a time. Keep your head up and focus ahead. Avoid lifting the skis off the snow as you step. Try not to shuffle; aim for large strides, gliding with each step. Glide on the forward foot and push off with the rear one.

Now repeat the exercise, this time using poles. As each leg advances in step, move the opposite pole forwards, planting it in the snow level with the heel of the lead foot. The pole should be angled back from your hand to help push you along. Keep your upper body relaxed. The movement is natural – the same alternate arm and leg motion used when walking without skis.

Figs 19(a) and (b)   The basic stance. You are ready for action, but relaxed, with ankles and knees slightly bent and weight evenly distributed on both feet. The skis are hip width apart.

Fig 20   Walking. As you slide each ski, move the opposite pole forwards, planting it in the snow level with the heel of the lead foot.

TURNING AROUND

Change direction in place by moving the tips of your skis apart and stepping around. Alternately, turn around by moving the ski tails instead of tips, in the same manner. The key is to move only the tips *or* tails to any degree, not both at once. Do this by raising the end in question marginally off the snow before moving it with a pivot of your ankle. This prevents crossing one ski over the other.

Figs 21(a–d)   Turn around.

Fig 21(a)
Change direction
in place by
moving the tips of
your skis apart and
stepping around.

Fig 21(d)
Continue
turning around.
To avoid
sliding
forwards, place
both poles
forward of your
feet, again
supporting
your weight on
the palms of
your hands.

Fig 21(b) and (c)   To avoid sliding backwards on a slope, place both poles behind you. Support your weight on the palms of your hands, with outstretched arms.

Figs 22 and 23   Sidestepping.

Moving one ski at a time, step sideways up the hill.

CLIMBING

There are two basic methods of ascending a slope: sidestepping and the herringbone. While both these movements can feel impossible at first, a little persistence soon pays off. The herringbone and sidestep are essential to a skier's mobility.

Sidestepping

Sidestepping is particularly useful on steeper slopes.

Begin in the basic position, with your skis parallel to each other and perpendicular to the fall line (across the slope). Add to the position by inclining your knees and ankles into the slope so that your uphill ski edges grip the snow. It is essential to maintain this edge grip to prevent slipping sideways.

Now imagine that you are climbing stairs sideways. Moving one ski at a time, step sideways up the hill.

The common mistake is to begin with the skis appropriately angled across the slope but to lose the angle while ascending. Skis that are not kept across the fall line with each step will slide accordingly, taking you with them!

Lifting the weight of skis evenly with each step makes it easier to place them parallel and across the fall line as you ascend.

Tip Concentrate on your uphill ski. With each step, keep it across the fall line and edging into the snow. Your downhill leg will mimic the action.

The Herringbone

The herringbone method allows you to climb straight up a gentle incline. The pattern left in the snow

Fig 24   Herringbone. Angle the inside edge of the skis into the snow. Using your knees to maintain grip, feel the pressure on your shin bones. As when walking, move the opposite hand and foot.

22

resembles a fish skeleton, hence the name.

Place the tails of your skis close together and the tips wide apart to form a large wedge. Now bring your weight forwards and angle the skis' inside edges into the snow. Use your knees to maintain this edge grip and feel the pressure on your shin bones. As when walking, move the opposite hand and foot while climbing up the fall line.

Most of the pressure should be on the arches and balls of your feet, but poles can be used to avoid sliding backwards. Place both poles behind you, with outstretched arms, and palms over the top instead of around the grip. Locking your elbows close to your torso distributes the load more evenly, should you need a rest.

STRAIGHT RUNNING

Gliding straight down the fall line on a gentle slope teaches you to balance on skis while in motion. A gentle, open slope, finishing in a slight incline or counterslope, is ideal for this exercise as it allows you to coast easily to a stop. Choose a quiet location away from other skiers if possible.

Sidestep up the slope a very short distance. Place your poles near the front of your skis to keep you from sliding forwards and move the tails of both skis behind you and up the hill.

Stand in a ready position, with feet shoulder width apart. Relax, and balance on the balls of both feet. Flex your ankles and knees, pressing your shins against the front of your boots. Look ahead, down the hill.

Now take your poles out of the snow and allow your skis to slide forwards. In the correct position

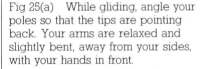

Figs 25(a) and (b)   Straight running. A gentle, open slope, finishing in a slight incline, is ideal for this exercise. A change in gradient allows you to coast easily to a stop.

Fig 25(a)   While gliding, angle your poles so that the tips are pointing back. Your arms are relaxed and slightly bent, away from your sides, with your hands in front.

Fig 25(b)   Keep your upper body upright and your eyes focused some distance ahead. Ankles, knees and hips should all be slightly flexed, with shins pressing against the front of your boots.

it is surprisingly easy to stay in balance over your skis. Don't be anxious; the flat runout or counterslope will bring you to a stop.

Remember, your ankles, knees and hips are slightly flexed, with the upper body upright and open (not hunched). Arms are kept slightly bent, out from the sides and with hands in front. Hold the poles with their tips pointing back, off the snow. Smile – your first glide should be fun!

Repeat the exercise several times, marginally increasing the height of your starting point as confidence develops.

GLIDING EXERCISES

In addition to gliding in the proper position, it can be helpful to experiment with other stances. Try balancing on one ski for a moment, being very tall or very low, or leaning far forwards and backwards. Exercises such as these develop feeling for the correct neutral, balanced position.

Balancing on one Leg

Alternately lifting one ski off the snow and then the other while straight running is a useful exercise for developing balance. Begin in your basic position with skis pointing down the fall line (the same slope as for straight running). Glide down the fall line, alternately lifting up the tail of each ski for a count of two. Move your weight over the ski on the snow to maintain balance.

Leaning Forwards and Backwards

To find a neutral, balanced position, lean far forwards and back against your boots for a moment, while straight running.

High and Low

Stand as tall as you can, then as low as possible, as you slide down the training slope. *Remember to look ahead!*

Fresh tracks in Verbier.

THE SNOWPLOUGH

The snowplough is an essential basic position, used for both turning and braking in the initial stages of skiing.

A good snowplough position equips the novice skier with a safe and reliable means of mobility. It is most relevant, however, in providing a base for more advanced moves.

Avoid developing a dependency on the snowplough as your sole means of stopping or turning. Instead, regard the snowplough as a useful catalyst for your future progression. The following snowplough exercises begin by developing a feel for the position and how it works in motion, before applying it as both a braking and full turning manoeuvre in the final exercises.

Fig 26   Snowplough or wedge position.

The Snowplough Position

The snowplough is so called because of the V shape formed by skis in this position. Ski tips are close together, while tails are pushed apart, resembling a plough or wedge. Skis rest on their inside edge, body weight is distributed evenly over both feet, and shins press against the front of your boots.

SNOWPLOUGH EXERCISES

Placing Skis in a Wedge

On flat terrain, step your skis, one at a time, into the wedge shape, then back to the straight running (parallel skis) position. Next, try hopping both skis simultaneously into the wedge position and back again. Lastly, practise sliding your skis into the snowplough. Simultaneously pivot both heels outwards so that ski tails slide apart into the wedge.

Using the Snowplough in Motion

Once you are able to slide skis into a wedge, you are ready to use the snowplough in motion. Practise moving skis from straight running to snowplough (and back) while sliding down a very gentle slope with a flat runout.

... Fig 27(c) snowplough, while gently sliding. Simultaneously pivot both heels outwards so that the ski tails slide apart into the wedge, and glide to a stop.

Figs 27(a–c)   Snowplough exercise. Using the snowplough in motion.

... Fig 27(b) straight running to ...

Fig 27(a)   Hold yourself back with the poles until you are ready. Practise moving your skis from ...

Figs 28(a) and (b)   A slight turn in motion.

Fig 28(a)   During a snowplough turn, the right foot is used to steer to the left.

Fig 28(b)   The left foot is used to steer to the right.

SLIGHT TURNS

It is important for future progress to make rhythmic turns before learning to brake. On the correct gentle terrain, stopping will not be a problem.

Skis in the snowplough position are already partially turned, so changing direction is simplified. Here's how.

As long as skis are held in a wedge, placing more weight over one ski will turn that ski in the direction it is pointing in. Place your weight over your left foot to steer to the right and your right foot to steer to the left – it's that simple. Don't sit back in the snowplough. In the correct body position, shins continually press against and flex the front of your boots.

Begin this exercise on a gentle gradient with a smooth runout (the same slope as for previous exercises).

Place skis in a small wedge before moving and, as with other manoeuvres, hold yourself back with your poles until ready to go.

Maintain the snowplough position while gliding. Now make gradual changes of direction by rhythmically alternating pressure from one foot to the other. Coast to a stop. For increased momentum, start slightly higher up the slope after each descent.

Spending a little extra time at this stage pays off later. The best thing you can do for rapid progress is to develop rhythmic turns before concerning yourself with the snowplough braking manoeuvre – braking is a blocking move, not a flowing one. Continue on this easy terrain until you feel capable with this exercise.

Tip For smooth turns, use a small wedge. A narrow wedge is easy to steer and will not slow you down too much. Feel weight pressing on to skis through your knees. Remember to relax, keep your head up, eyes looking ahead. Steer with your feet, not with your upper body.

THE SNOWPLOUGH STOP

The 'wedge' shape of skis in the snowplough position works as a brake by providing resistance to the gravitational pull of the fall line. Now that you have achieved a feeling for the snowplough as a turning manoeuvre, learning the snowplough stop is a small and easy step.

Exercise 1

Use the same gentle slope as in the previous exercise. Start in the straight running position; begin gliding a short distance and check your basic stance (ankles and knees flexed, upper body open and relaxed, not hunched over and closed in). Glide far enough to gain momentum before brushing your skis out into the snowplough with a positive pushing out movement of both heels. The pivoting effort of your feet must be maintained to hold the

wedge shape of skis constant and effect a stop.

Repeat the exercise and develop the feeling. Your snowplough will effect a stop in shorter distances as efforts improve.

Exercise 2

Start slightly higher up the slope. Practise descending, alternately putting on and releasing the brakes by changing skis from a snowplough

Fig 29   A snowplough turning exercise. Alternate pressure from one foot to the other to make gentle, rhythmic turns down the slope. Use a small wedge!

to a straight running position. Concentrate on a 'even' wedge to avoid deviations or turns from the fall line. One leg is often weaker than the other to begin with. Skiing is an ambidextrous sport – we must learn to use both sides of our body equally.

SNOWPLOUGH TURN EXERCISES

Now that you can use the snowplough to make gradual rhythmic turns and stop, it's time to put these newly learned skills into effect. The point of the following exercises is to fully develop the ability to steer by linking complete turns across the fall line. Practise on a gentle slope where excessive braking will not be required.

Linked Snowplough Turns

To make larger turns, use the same transfer of weight as during partial turns, but increase the time that each ski is pressured. Glide across the same slope as before in a snowplough position and steer towards the fall line by turning your upper body in the direction of the turn and pressuring the outside ski.

Now maintain the turning action by pushing the flexed outside knee forwards and inwards. This increases the edge angle on the turning ski. Hips and upper body face slightly down the hill.

The motion of flexing and extending ankles, knees and hips is continual as you descend, and necessary for every turn. Gradually

flex ankles and knees (go lower) just before turning to create a 'platform' from which to rise, then extend (rise) to begin the turn. Flex your ankles and knees again to finish the turn, creating a 'platform' for the following turn.

Snowplough Slalom Exercise

Using markers to turn around is useful in developing rhythm and pressure control. Place several poles 'slalom like' in a row, and practise skiing through them with rounded, linked turns. This will improve the rhythm of your turns. Practise this without your poles in hand to improve your position and balance on skis.

Move your upper body over the

Figs 30(a–c)   The snowplough stop.

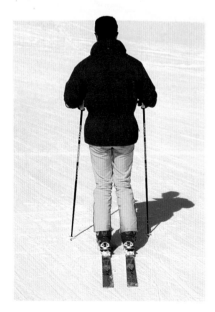

Fig 30(a)   Start in the straight running position.

Fig 30(b)   Brush your skis out into the snowplough with a positive pushing-out movement of both heels.

Fig 30(c)   Maintain pushing pressure in the heels until you stop.

Figs 31(a–c)   A snowplough slalom exercise.

In photo (c), he is pressuring the right ski to turn left.

In photo (b), Kusan is pressuring his left ski to turn right.

Make round turns through a 'slalom' course made from ski poles.

outside, turning ski, the ski further from the turn marker, to increase pressure on it. Remember to flex your ankles at the beginning and end of each turn.

Touching the Outside Knee

The following exercise emphasizes the movement of your upper body to the outside of the turn and the feeling of concentrating pressure on the inside edge of the outside ski.

Reach down and touch your outside knee with your outside hand. Make several turns, alternately touching each knee as the turn is initiated. The left hand touches the left knee when turning right, and the right hand touches the right knee when turning left.

Fig 32   Touching outside knee. Reach down and touch your outside knee with your outside hand. Make several rhythmic turns, touching the left knee when turning right and the right knee when turning left.

Figs 33(a)–(c)   Linked snowplough turns. Practise linking large, round, snowplough turns.

Fig 33(a)   While turning, lower your stance to increase pressure on the outside ski. Push the flexed knee forwards towards the inside of the turn. (Push against the front of your ski boot.)

Fig 33(b)   Gradually rise between turns.

CHECKPOINTS TO REMEMBER

1   A strong snowplough will be difficult to initiate and maintain if weight is not over your knees.
2   In the correct body position, shins continually press against and flex the front of your boots.
3   Your upper body moves to the outside of the turn.

Anxious beginners often neglect the points above and unknowingly adopt a backward-leaning, passive stance when trying new moves. Overcome this by continually checking that your pelvis is not weighted back in a 'sitting' position and that shins are pressing forwards against the front of your boots.

Fig 33(c)   Steer towards the fall line by turning your upper body in the direction of the turn and pressing on the foot that is on the outside of the turn.

Fig 34   The rounder the turn, the smoother the ride.

TRAVERSING

Traversing is simply skiing across the fall line. For the beginner, traversing is one of the first and best ways of controlling speed. Speed is governed by the angle of the traverse to the fall line.

Skis positioned at right angles to the fall line will be motionless. Taking that position a few degrees lower makes for a slow and gentle traverse. This is known as a shallow traverse.

Skis angled progressively closer to the fall line traverse at increased speeds. This type of traverse is called a steep traverse.

Learning the correct traverse position early in skiing develops edge control and balance/stance, and leaves little room for bad habits to form.

At first, traversing in the correct stance may feel uncomfortable. This position is called 'angulated'; perhaps the name says it all. Ease comes with practice. Your ability to maintain this 'angulated' position will improve progressively as you ski steeper terrain.

Practise traversing in both directions, especially in the direction that you find more difficult; it is normal to find some manoeuvres easier to do in one direction than the other. Overcome this by working on your weaker side – skiing demands equal skills of both sides of your body.

The Traverse Position

A gentle slope with firm snow is recommended for your first attempts at traversing.

Place greater weight over the downhill ski than the uphill ski. Bring the uphill ski slightly forwards of the downhill one. (Weight distribution and placing of skis compen-

Fig 35   Traversing. Ski across a smooth, gentle slope. If necessary, move the tails of your skis uphill slightly to begin moving.

sates for slope gradient.) Gently flex ankles, knees and hips and press shins against the front of your boots. Incline your knees and ankles into the uphill slope so that uphill ski edges are in contact with and grip the snow. Modify the amount of knee/ankle inclination to the steepness of slope. Angulate your upper body towards the fall line, holding your arms out to the side and hands in front. Look ahead in the direction of traverse, and relax.

In the correct position, all uphill parts of the body (shoulder, hip, leg, foot, etc.) will be slightly forward of their downhill counterpart.

TRAVERSING EXERCISES

The following balance exercises help you to feel the balance point on the lower ski. Remember that

Fig 36   Traverse on the downhill ski. Lift the tail of your uphill ski several times while traversing. Hold it up for a count of three before putting it back on the snow.

the lower ski must be predominantly weighted. Once you are able to hold the traverse without slipping sideways, practise joining traverses with snowplough turns and create an unbroken line of tracks zig-zagging down the slope.

Fig 37 Pedal traverse. Traverse across a gentle slope, alternately picking up each ski for a count of two (like pedalling a bike across the hill). Notice the track left in the snow. This exercise trains you to change pressure from downhill ski to uphill and to balance on the uphill foot – essential for advanced turns.

Fig 38 Touching the downhill knee with the uphill hand moves your uphill hip forward into the correct position for traversing. Anna Marie Bruechert demonstrates.

Fig 39 Hold your poles horizontally with both hands (like carrying a tray), with the poles parallel over your downhill ski. This ensures angulation of the upper body.

STEPPING UPHILL TO STOP

Stepping uphill is a safe method of coming to a stop or changing direction while crossing a slope. Stepping uphill to stop also teaches you how to shift your weight from ski to ski. This exercise is a development of the 'pedal' traverse exercise.

Practise first on the flat; take small steps, moving the tips of your skis apart. (The movement is the same as when you first learned to turn around on the flat.)

Then sidestep a little way up the slope scissoring ski tips apart as you step uphill. Use small steps with tips of skis moving slightly uphill of the tails.

Finally practise stepping uphill while traversing. As your traverse becomes shallower you will glide to a stop.

Fig 40(a)   Begin in a shallow traverse.

Figs 40(a)–(d)   Stepping uphill to stop.

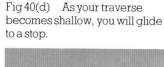

Figs 40(b)–(c)   Scissor ski tips apart to step uphill.

Fig 40(d)   As your traverse becomes shallow, you will glide to a stop.

SKI LIFTS
Riding Lifts

Begin using lifts to ride to the top of the beginner's slope as soon as possible after learning to turn and stop. Lifts save you time and energy for the most fun part of skiing, going down the hill! Using lifts gives you the opportunity to acquire mileage on skis – so important at this stage.

Lifts on beginners' slopes vary in type from one resort to the next. Your first ride may be on a handle tow, poma, T-bar or chairlift. Whichever it is, all lifts, if used correctly, allow you to rest and relax between runs.

Poma lifts and T-bars are most common for beginners in European resorts. Both of these lifts require that you support your own weight; stand, rather than sit, as you ride them. Use the basic stance, lean into the front of your boots and allow the lift to pull you up the hill. Neither lift is designed to be sat on, pulling or sitting back on the lift causes the bar to give like elastic, depositing unwary skiers on the snow in the process.

Most North American resorts favour chairlifts. When loading on to a chairlift, hold ski poles in one hand and catch the chair with the other. This will prevent the chair from banging you as it slides beneath your bottom.

Sit down promptly and close the safety barrier, if there is one. Remove the safety barrier shortly before arriving at the summit and prepare to stand up and ski away on arrival.

POMA LIFTS: The Poma (or button) lift consists of a simple disk on the end of a metal bar attached to a moving cable. The disk goes between your legs and rests against your bottom to pull you up the hill.

Hold onto the bar for balance but let the button do the pulling.

The pomas gather at the bottom of the lift and are released automatically when you pass through the loading area.

Hold poles in one hand and the poma in the other. Let the poma pull you up the slope. Don't sit on the poma or practise turning while going up the track – pulling the cable to the side may cause it to derail – making you very unpopular with the lift operator!

T-BAR LIFTS: T-bars work on a similar principle to pomas but are made to be ridden by two persons. Instead of a single disk the upright bar is attached to a horizontal piece, the two making the shape of an upside down letter T, so that a skier can ride either side.

As you come close to the lift, transfer both poles to your (free) outside hand. Slide into the loading area once the previous skier has gone.

Look over your inside shoulder towards the approaching T-bar.

Take the centre of the T-bar with your inside hand as it passes between you and your partner, placing the crossbar beneath your bottom. Remember, don't sit down! Keep ankles and knees flexed and let it pull you up the hill. Looking ahead will help you stay in the track.

If you should fall, don't hold on! Let go of the T and remove yourself from the track before snowploughing back down to the loading area.

Be ready to unload as you near the top of the lift. Look ahead to note direction to ski away (the direction of exit will be indicated by signs, rope fences or general traffic).

Remove the T-bar by pulling it back slightly then away from you, and let go. Release it gently, without letting it swing, to avoid damaging the T or possibly derailing it.

Now move quickly away from the unloading area; watch out for others that have failed to do so.

Figs 41 and 42   Riding a poma lift.

Figs 43 and 44   Riding a T-bar.

Fig 43   Hold both poles in your outside hand when you are loading onto a T-bar.

Fig 44   This T-bar services an excellent beginners' slope on the Gentianes glacier in Verbier, Switzerland. The cable car in the distance provides access to steeper terrain on Mont Fort.

Fig 45   Reading the lift map.

Fig 46   The Mont Fort cable car in Verbier.

Handle Tows

Handle tows consist of individual handles attached to a moving cable. As there is no spring to absorb shock, these provide an initial pull – be prepared! Luckily these usually move quite slowly and are not really that hard to catch on to for a ride up the slope.

Chairlifts

Chairlifts are slightly different because you ride sitting down. When getting on a chairlift, be sure to watch its approach and use your free hand to catch it slightly to avoid a nasty bump on the back of the leg. Sit down immediately, keeping your skis tracking in a straight line until they leave the snow. Close the safety bar if there is one.

Move the safety bar out of the way as you approach the top of the lift. Keep your skis straight and ski tips up, letting them slide for a second on the snow before standing up and skiing away from the unloading area.

Lift Maps

Always obtain a map of the lift system before going up the mountain. In addition to providing a guide to lifts and trails, the area map usually includes a list of mountain restaurants, lift closing times, and safety advice such as the location of first-aid posts.

Fig 47(a)   A handle tow.

Fig 47(b)   A chairlift. Nicky Legrand and Balou are riding.

CAT TRACKS

Cat tracks are gentle trails that wind down the mountain. Once you are able to snowplough turn and stop, use cat tracks to avoid difficult terrain. The name comes from snowcat – not an animal, but a machine used to groom snow.

Trail Markers

Beginners should pay special attention to the trail-marking system. Coloured markers at the start of each trail correspond to its degree of difficulty. The colours used vary between countries. Switzerland, for example, marks the easiest runs with blue signposts, intermediate trails with red and the most difficult trails with black. Check the lift/piste map to be clear on a resort's colour-coding system.

Additional signs, flags and symbols are used for safety and to help you find your way around. At most areas, these are featured on the map. Pay special attention to 'trail closed' signs. These are put up for your benefit and should not be ignored. For example after heavy snowfalls, and on spring afternoons, it is often necessary to close tracks that pass beneath slopes prone to avalanche.

Note Trailside markers (used to find your way during bad visibility) can be seen on the right of the cat track on page 103.

3 Beyond Basics

THE FAN PROGRESSION

A fan progression is the simplest way to build confidence while progressing from the snowplough to a basic parallel turn.

With a fan progression, one turn is done at a time. You progress from shallow turns made across the hill, to rounder turns starting in the fall line. The radius of the turn is gradually increased each time.

The initial exercise is sideslipping/ edging (a controlled skid on uphill ski edges). The next stage is learning to christie (a single skidded turn) up the hill. The chapter ends with linked basic parallel turns (turning with skis parallel to one another) on a gentle slope.

HOW SKIS WORK

Skis turn because of their shape and the way that they flex under pressure. They are narrower in the waist than at each end; this is called sidecut. Skis also have camber: lying on a flat surface, a ski touches only at the tip and tail. When a skier stands on a ski, camber causes weight to be distributed equally along the bottom. While turning, weight is concentrated under the centre of the ski, causing its camber to be reversed (bent the other way).

Reversing the camber of a ski has two effects. Firstly, bending increases the effect of sidecut – pressing harder on an edged ski causes it to turn more sharply.

Secondly, reversing the camber causes the ski to act as a spring when pressure is removed. The rebound effect is similar to that which a diver derives from a springboard.

Skis also twist when pressure is applied to the edge. The amount that a ski twists is termed torsional resistance. A ski with little torsional resistance will be forgiving but will also wash out easily on hard snow.

New materials and construction techniques permit designers to make skis that are extremely narrow in the waist (usually narrower than the width of a ski boot), softer flexing longitudinally and stiffer torsionally than in the past. These factors combine to make the best skis turn

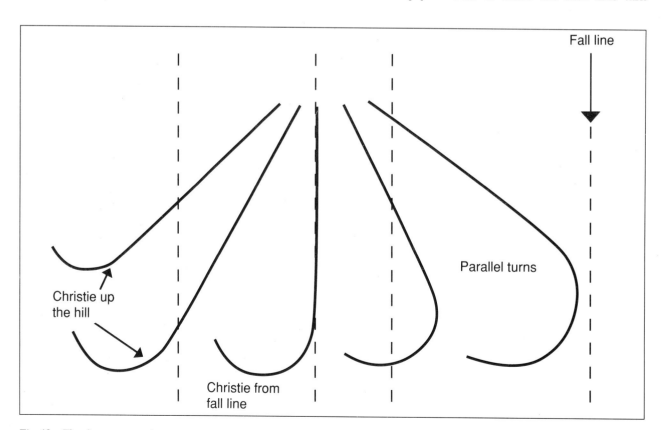

Fig 48   The fan progression.

38

easily and grip the snow tenaciously. Skiing is more effortless now than in the past; extreme body movements are no longer necessary to turn a ski.

TERRAIN

Don't be pressured by well-meaning friends into skiing slopes beyond your ability. Stay on easy trails to develop technique and build a solid foundation in the basic skills. Successfully learning a new manoeuvre requires a consistent development of a few positive, fluid movements. Steeper trails force excessive braking, and make for defensive skiing. This results in poor technique and hurts long-term progress. It is easy to overestimate your ability after a good day on easy terrain. Being patient now will save you time and frustration later. However, while 'getting out of your depth' is not recommended, a gradual increase in steepness actually makes turning skis easier.

SIDESLIPPING/EDGING

Sideslipping allows you to move sideways in a controlled slide down the fall line. Sideslipping provides an easy, safe method of descending slopes that you feel are too steep, narrow, icy or rocky to ski. Ski edges are used to control the skid.

A steep slope is necessary to sideslip easily. Use the bottom of a suitable slope and sidestep up a short distance. Firm snow facilitates skidding.

The stance for sideslipping is identical to that of traversing. The 'angulated' position controls the skis' edges. Edge skis to make them grip the snow, and roll skis off their edges to permit sideslipping.

Fig 49   Sideslipping. A controlled slide down the fall line.

Here is a quick reminder of the traverse position:

1   Place more weight on the downhill ski than on the uphill one.
2   Place the uphill ski slightly ahead of the downhill ski.
3   Balance on the uphill edge of both skis, pushing against the front of your boots.
4   Press hips and knees into the hill and face your upper body down the fall line, with arms apart and hands in front.

A Sideslipping Exercise

Sidestep a short distance up the slope and stop for a moment, balanced on the uphill edge of both skis.

Now roll both knees and ankles away from the hill. This will release the skis' uphill edges. As you feel the edges release, initiate sliding by pushing the lower ski sideways and allow the upper ski to follow, parallel to the lower. Feel your edges brushing the snow while sideslipping.

To stop sliding, flex your ankles and roll your knees back towards the slope so that the skis' uphill edges grip the snow. This motion, called 'setting the edge' or an 'edge set', is crucial in advanced skiing – practise accordingly!

Note Practise sideslipping in both directions and letting your skis slide more freely before setting the edges.

Figs 50(a)–(d) Sideslipping exercise.

Fig 50(a) Balance on the uphill edges of both skis.

Fig 50(b) Roll both knees away from the slope to initiate sliding.

Fig 50(c) Feel your edges brushing the snow.

Fig 50(d) Flex your ankles and roll your knees back towards the slope, 'setting' the edge and stopping the slide.

DIAGONAL SIDESLIP

Diagonal sideslipping, also called a directional sideslip, falls somewhere between sideslipping and traversing. This combination is the first stage of our fan progression. The movement required is similar to that necessary in initiating a 'christie' or sliding turn (your next major goal).

Find a short, moderate-grade slope with firm snow. The angle of a moderate gradient makes it easier to release edges than a gentle gradient does.

Tip Beginners often find it difficult to grasp the idea of simultaneously crossing and sliding down a slope. The solution is to visualize traversing with skis slightly flattened.

Stand in your traverse position, and choose a destination point across and down the slope. Roll your ankles and knees very slightly downhill so that your edges are only just gripping. Now, as you move, your skis will slide downhill as you ski across the slope. Relax in a stable position. Control the degree of slide by lightly edging, and head towards your destination point.

(Edging more, rolling your knees and ankles towards the slope, stops drifting and puts you back on a traverse or stops you.)

Tips 1. Maintain even pressure against the front of your ski boots. 2. As when traversing normally, balance most of your weight over the arch of your downhill foot.

Figs 51(a) and (b)   Diagonal sideslip.

Fig 51(a)   Relax in a stable position; control the slide by edging lightly.

Fig 51(b)   Diagonal sideslip viewed from behind.

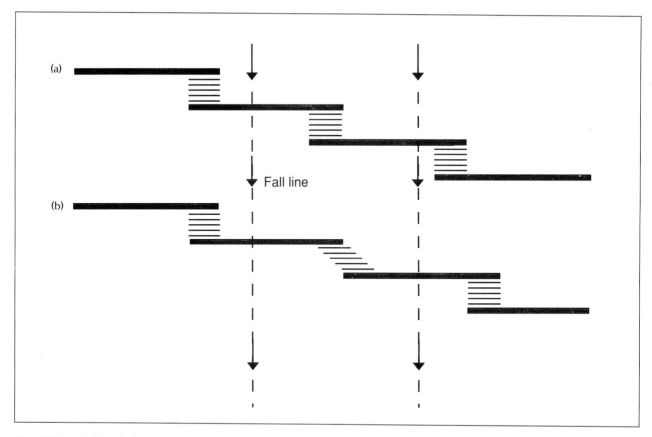

Figs 52(a) and (b)   Staircase sideslip.   (a) The track left in the snow resembles a staircase profile.
(b) Switching between sideslipping, traversing and directional sideslipping to further test your skill.

The Staircase Sideslip Exercise

Staircase sideslipping alternates traversing and sideslipping as you cross the slope. When this exercise is done correctly, the track left resembles a staircase profile.

This exercise trains subtle foot movements, fine tuning your edging skills. In addition to being a great exercise for beginning skiers, staircase sideslipping is also an effective remedial exercise for intermediate skiers who use excessive upper-body movement. The upper body should be quiet while sideslipping – all of the 'action' takes place below the hip.

Begin by traversing. After sliding two or three metres (6½–10ft), release your edges to sideslip down the slope two or three metres, then roll you knees back into the hill to continue traversing. Alternate traversing and sideslipping across the slope. Then repeat in the opposite direction.

Tip   For variety and as a test of skill, switch between straight sideslipping and diagonal sideslipping.

Note   Many intermediate skiers, in the habit of using their hips to throw skis around, miss the fine footwork that is the key to advanced skiing. Staircase sideslipping may be tricky at first, but perfecting this man-oeuvre now prevents many technical problems later.

THE GLIDE CHRISTIE UP THE HILL

The glide christie up the hill is the first stage on the way to learning to turn with skis parallel. It's a partial turn across the slope that trains you to bring skis parallel at the completion of the turn. This exercise is a continuation of directional sideslipping.

You may have discovered while learning to sideslip that on steeper slopes, skis slide easily across the fall line. Use a part of the slope that is *slightly* steeper than where you began the snowploughing exercises. You will find that the uphill ski slides easily parallel as long as you release the wedge.

Begin turning towards the fall line in a gliding snowplough and gradually turn the uphill or inside ski parallel to the outside ski. Flex slightly as you cross the slope in a skidded arc. The outside ski steers continuously.

Tip Relax and concentrate on using your lower body to steer your skis; the upper body is just going along for the ride.

Note A little extra speed simplifies pivoting. Increase the angle of your traverse, a little steeper each time until you start in the fall line. Alternate left and right turns of the same

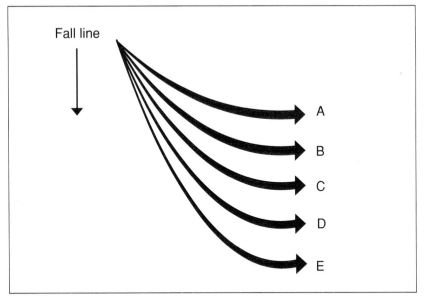

Fig 54   Increase the angle of your traverse a little steeper each time until you are starting in the fall line.

Figs 53(a)–(c) Glide christie up the hill.

Fig 53(a)   From a shallow traverse, slide tails apart to form a small wedge. Begin steering the downhill, outside ski towards the fall line.

Fig 53(b)   Gradually slide the uphill ski parallel with the downhill ski.

Fig 53(c)   Flex slightly and glide uphill to a stop.

43

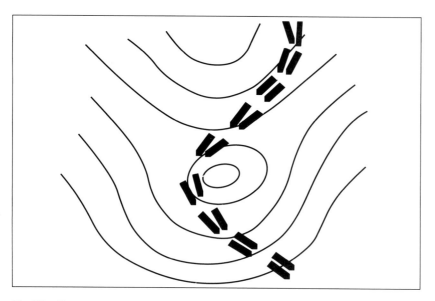

Fig 55   Convex terrain makes it easy to slide the inside ski parallel.

In a narrow snowplough, steer towards the fall line then steer back into a traverse. Bring the skis parallel as you steer them back into the traverse (as you did in the christie up the hill), but don't stop. Repeat as you cross the slope.

Slightly steeper terrain makes it easier to bring skis parallel. As you know from traversing, it is easy to control speed while crossing a slope by turning more up the hill. A christie garland lets you experiment with completing your turns in a parallel position without going too fast.

LINKED GLIDE CHRISTIES

Practising the glide christie brings the skier one step closer to the parallel turn.

A glide christie is a complete turn across the fall line that begins in a snowplough wedge and finishes with skis parallel in a traverse position. Here's how it works.

Initiate the turn in a snowplough wedge and maintain the wedge to the point where skis turn through the fall line. Then release the plough by sliding the uphill ski parallel to the downhill ski. Finish the turn with skis momentarily across the slope in the traverse position. Initiate the following turn by opening skis back into a snowplough wedge and repeat the manoeuvre.

Aim at bringing the skis together sooner with each new turn. On slightly steeper terrain, you have only to release the inside ski of its plough and it will automatically slide parallel. Let the slope do the work!

To prepare for turning from a shallow traverse, flex your ankles and knees and slide the skis into a small wedge. Begin to turn your upper body to face down the slope.

radius: it's normal to be able to turn better in one direction than the other – training both sides of your body at the same pace ensures smooth progress.

THE CHRISTIE GARLAND

A christie garland is a series of linked partial turns across the slope. Properly executed, the exercise leaves a track in the snow resembling a garland or necklace.

Fig 56   The christie garland.

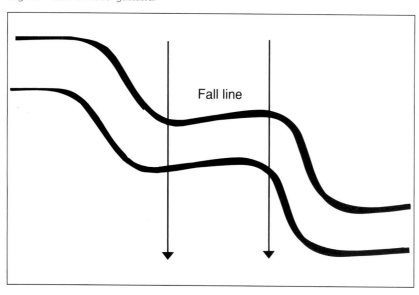

Fall line

Figs 57(a)–(e)   Glide christies.

Fig 57(a)

Fig 57(b)

Fig 57(c)

Fig 57(d)

Extend your ankles and knees, and steer the uphill, outside ski into the fall line. Gradually slide the inside ski parallel with the outside ski. To complete the turn, continue steering your skis completely across the fall line, pressing your shins against the front of your boots, towards the inside of the turn. Slide your skis into a small wedge to prepare for the next turn.

Note Notice the down-up-down motion through Lisa's turn. Lisa stands lower to begin the turn, taller

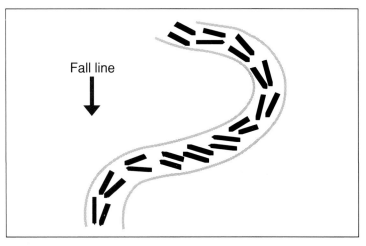

Fall line

Fig 57(e)

45

through its apex and lower again to complete the turn. The positions for beginning and ending the turn are identical. This flexion and extension movement (similarly used in your snowplough exercises) works to momentarily lighten skis at the crucial point in turning. The relevance of flexion and extension increases as we head towards parallel turns and is further explained with developments through the rest of this chapter.

Remember, speed is controlled by the radius of your turns, not by using the wedge to brake. To descend more slowly, keep skis turning for longer.

Tip Always try to make turns as *round* as possible; don't rush. A *gradual* increase in flexion and edging is needed to steer and edge your skis.

THE ELEMENTARY CHRISTIE AND POLE PLANT

If you've been curious until now about what to do with your poles, here's the answer. The elementary christie exercise trains you to use your poles correctly. It's a sliding turn, using a pole plant to trigger the beginning of the turn. This manoeuvre is also commonly called a 'stem christie'. It's an exaggerated manoeuvre; use the elementary christie to learn how to use your poles, not as an end goal.

Rhythm is an essential part of skiing and evolves as you develop coordination of movement with the motion of skiing. So far your poles have only been used to aid mobility. Poles are primarily a timing device. When and how you plant them affects your turns. Poles provide a beat with which to keep rhythm.

Figs 58(a)–(f) The pole plant (elementary christie). Kusan Staubli demonstrates.

Fig 58(a) Sink low, opening your skis into a small wedge.

Fig 58(b) Plant your ski pole in the snow and rise, steering the outside ski towards the fall line. Rising puts your body in a balanced, forward position, anticipating your movement down the slope.

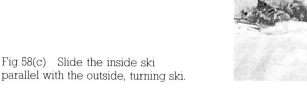

Fig 58(c) Slide the inside ski parallel with the outside, turning ski.

Practise the pole plant first while straight running, before progressing to the elementary christie. Use a gentle slope where you can glide comfortably. Slowly descend while rhythmically flexing and extending your ankles with a down-up-down motion. Keep both hands forward and relaxed. Trigger extension by touching the snow with the tip of your pole – the pole plant. Use only your wrist and lower arm to swing the pole – keep the upper arm and shoulder relaxed. Practise until you are comfortable with the rhythm of rising as you plant your pole.

Now on a slightly steeper part of the slope, practise coordinating the pole plant with turning. The ideal terrain will be almost flat on top, gradually becoming steeper (not too steep!). This allows you to develop some rhythm in advance of the slope.

On the top section, alternately plant your poles as you begin the rising motion. As the slope steepens, use the rising motion (extension) to initiate turns and emphasize the movement. Synchronizing the pole plant in action takes time to get right; relax and be patient, don't force it. Feel it.

Remember, a well-timed pole plant is the key to smooth, rhythmic, advanced skiing – practise accordingly.

Fig 58(e)   Plant the pole and rise, steering the new outside ski into the turn.

Fig 58(d)   As you move lower to finish the turn, open your skis into a wedge again and prepare to plant the opposite pole to trigger the following turn.

Fig 58(f)   Slide the new inside ski parallel with the outside.

THE BASIC PARALLEL TURN

Parallel turns (turning without using a stem or wedge) are smoother, more dynamic, and quicker than turns using a stem or wedge. The secret to parallel turns is to harmonize the pivoting of both feet with unweighting – making your skis lighter on the snow.

When learning parallel turns, begin with one turn at a time, as during the glide christie exercise. Increase the radius of each turn until you are able to start in the fall line. Finally, connect a few turns back and forth across the fall line.

By now you are familiar with the concept of flexion and extension as an unweighting manoeuvre. But flexion and extension does more than unweight skis in advanced stages of skiing. Here's how it works with the parallel turn.

Flexion means to flex or bend ankles and knees. During a basic parallel turn, flexion increases pressure on the ski, the counterpoint to unweighting. Adding pressure to a ski on edge pushes it against the snow, causing it to counter-flex and resist sideways motion. Flexion is necessary at the beginning and end of a basic parallel turn to create a 'platform' from which to rise into the next turn.

Extension means to straighten legs. Extending makes skis momentarily light on the snow and easy to pivot. Your extension should be forward, toward the fall line and not straight up. During the fleeting moment that your skis are light on the snow, they are easy to steer away from their original direction. At the same time, if you roll them slightly onto the edge that they are skidding on, steering is accentuated.

In certain conditions almost no unweighting is needed, for example on icy snow, where skis slip easily, and in moguls, where the shape of the bump is used to aid the pivoting of skis in the turn. For these conditions, maximum snow contact is the goal and excessive unweighting is to be avoided. The opposite applies in deep or heavy snow, where extra effort is needed. To improve parallel turning, avoid extreme conditions and moguls at first; practise on smoothly groomed intermediate runs.

Tip Always begin flexing from the *ankles*; feel your shins pushing up against the front of your boots.

Note Boots that are too stiff will be difficult to flex. Stiff boots are designed for greater speeds and need more force – and are not recommended for improving intermediate skills. A good boot flexes smoothly; avoid boots that suddenly stop flexing. Boots with uneven flex bruise shins and make smooth turns more difficult.

The effect of flexion and extension is easy to observe. Stand on some bathroom scales and flex and extend your ankles. Notice how your weight changes, becoming greater as you press on the scale to rise, and lighter when your ankles are fully extended.

THE PARALLEL TURN UP THE HILL

Practise on a smooth intermediate slope, one turn at a time. This allows you to break down the parallel turn into its parts: preparation, initiation and completion. (When linking turns, preparation and completion become the same thing.)

Prepare for the turn by flexing your ankles and knees. To begin turning, touch the snow with your pole, rise off your uphill foot and steer the skis out of the fall line. Flex down again and steer your skis across the slope to complete the turn.

The down-up-down motion created by flexing and extending reduces pressure on the bottom of your skis, making them easy to turn. This is known as up-unweighting.

Note Although Lisa is stopping here, her upper body is facing towards the fall line in preparation for another turn. Her position is described technically as 'anticipated' – prepared for the next turn – and 'angulated' – the upper body faces down the slope while knees press into the slope for edge control.

Figs 59(a)–(d) Parallel turn up the hill.

Fig 59(a) Preparation:
Flex your ankles and knees.

Fig 59(b) Initiation: Touch the
snow with a pole, rise off
the uphill foot and steer your
skis out of the fall line.

Fig 59(c) Completion: Flex
again and steer the skis across
the slope to complete the turn.
The uphill, outside foot becomes
the downhill foot at completion
of the turn.

Fig 59(d) Come to a stop by
continuing to turn up the
hill.

49

Figs 60(a)–(f)   The parallel turn.

Fig 60(a)   Flex your ankles and knees.

Fig 60(b)   Plant your pole and rise off your uphill, outside foot and steer the skis through the fall line.

Fig 60(c)   Steer the skis across the slope (more weight on the outside, downhill foot).

50

LINKED PARALLEL TURNS

The key to connecting turns is to build rhythm as you descend. Remember, the flexing movement needed to complete one turn prepares you for the next.

Pressure Control

The importance of pressure control in the parallel turn is not well illustrated in photographs. During a parallel turn, the transfer of pressure from one foot to the other follows the same basic principle as that used in a snowplough turn.

Remember, your outside ski is used to initiate and steer each turn. When you are turning, the outside ski is briefly the uphill ski, becoming the downhill ski as the skis pivot and complete the turn. It is here at the completion of one turn and the initiation of the next that the pressure transfer onto the new outside ski occurs.

Fig 60(d) Flex your ankles and knees and prepare to plant the pole.

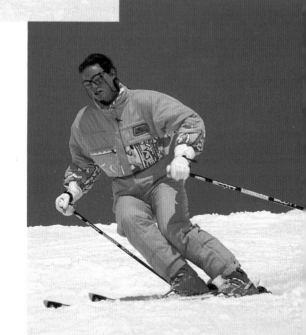

Fig 60(e) Plant the pole and extend off the uphill (outside) ski. Notice that the extension is forward and down the hill, not straight up.

Fig 60(f) Flex your ankles and knees to continue steering across the fall line and prepare for the following turn.

51

Skier Kusan Staubli.

KICKTURN

A kickturn works from a standing position and enables the skier to turn in the opposite direction in place. Fluid movements are needed for an effective kickturn.

Balance yourself with your poles and place all of your weight on one ski. Raise the other ski, swinging its tip up and forwards, and rest it on its tail. Practise this first to get the feeling of lifting your foot.

Now plant both poles behind your back for stable support, turn the lifted ski 180 degrees and put it back down on the snow. Follow with the outside ski and pole, and you are set to move off in the new direction.

Figs 61(a)–(e)   The kickturn.

Fig 61(a)   Plant both poles behind your back for stable support and place all your weight on the ski that is to be the outside of your turn.

Fig 61(b)   Lift the other ski, swinging it up and forwards and rest it on its tail.

Fig 61(c)   Turn the lifted ski 180 degrees, then put it back down on the snow.

Fig 61(d)   Follow with the outside ski and pole.

Fig 61(e)   Set to move off in the new direction.

SKATING

Skating allows you to move easily across the flat. Learning to skate is also a valuable exercise in its own right.

First practise skating without using any poles. Swing your hands alternately as when walking and ice skating (the left hand going forwards with the right foot and vice versa).

Push off the inside edge of one ski and move forwards onto the other to glide. The ski on which you are gliding becomes the pushing ski in the following stride.

Next, practise skating using your poles to assist propulsion. Push with both poles simultaneously to increase glide as you move onto the new ski.

Figs 62(a)–(c) Skating without poles.

Fig 62(a) Swing hands alternately. The left hand goes forward with the right foot.

Figs 63(a)–(e) Skating using poles. Push with both poles simultaneously to enhance gliding.

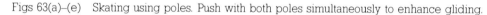

Fig 63(a)   Fig 63(b)   Fig 63(c)

Fig 62(b)   The right hand goes
forward with the left foot.

Fig 62(c)   Use momentum to glide as far as possible
on each foot.

Fig 63(d)

Fig 63(e)

4 Improving Techniques

So far you have progressed by developing your ability with a 'step-by-step' series of basic manoeuvres. Now it's time to look at the individual skills of skiing. This chapter works on developing and refining these skills, with the ultimate objective of helping intermediate skiers to breakthrough to an advanced level, as well as to improve and perfect the technique of advanced skiers.

Advanced skiers ski with energy, finesse and precision. If you are already advanced, work on the skills in this chapter and aim for greater consistency in performance.

LINE

Skiing, can be likened in one way to riding a motorcycle on a race track: you must look well ahead. Ski racers typically look at least two gates down the hill. In normal skiing your route is unmarked, but the same concentration is needed to direct yourself through a chosen line. Looking ahead gives you time to choose the optimum line and prepare for bumps, icy snow or changes in pitch.

Develop the habit of looking ahead by pushing yourself to concentrate more, and practise focusing two or three turns ahead. Try this: spot a good place to turn and head towards it, looking for your following turning point as you do so – its location will determine the radius of the approaching turn. And so on. Don't forget to take the actions of other skiers into consideration when choosing your line.

Fig 64(b)

Fig 64(c)

Fig 64(d)

Figs 64(a)–(d) Absorbing bumpy terrain. Traverse across the bumps, flexing both ankles as your skis run into the rise. Keep your hands forward and extend your legs into the trough on the other side.

BASIC MOGUL TECHNIQUE

Ski slopes don't stay smooth forever; bumps, or moguls, form in the snow when many skiers turn in the same spot. Even with slope-grooming machines, as long as there are skiers, there will always be bumps. As with every new ski technique, mastering moguls should be a steady, confidence-building process. Think of mogul runs as a playground, and have fun learning.

Absorbing Bumpy Terrain

Learn to ski moguls by developing the ability to absorb bumps in a traverse. Flexion and extension are the key to absorbing bumps and other obstacles. A skier without flexion will rocket off every bump like a tin man on wheels. The trick is to stay loose, and let your legs act as shock absorbers. As you ski over a bump, flex your ankles and knees to absorb the mound, then extend your legs into the hollow on the other side. These hollows or depressions in the snow are known as troughs. Pressing skis into the trough prepares you for absorbing the next bump. Avoid being stuck in one position, tall or low.

TERRAIN: Choose a gentle slope with a few bumps.

Fig 64(a)

Rolf Liechti.

Fig 65(a) Approach the mogul in a tall stance.

Figs 65(a)–(d) Pivoting on a mogul. Flex your ankles and knees to absorb the bump. Plant your pole and pivot both skis at the top of the bump. Stand tall as the skis slide into the trough on the other side to prepare to absorb the following mogul in the next turn.

Fig 65(b) Flex ankles and knees on the top of the mogul, planting your pole and pivoting both skis on the crest.

Turning on Moguls

If you are just beginning to ski moguls, the initial objective is to ski in control and descend a moderate mogul slope without stopping every few turns. This is not difficult, with a little practice, it is actually easier to turn on a mogul than on a perfectly smooth slope.

Begin by working on a single turn and gradually increase the number of turns without stopping. To control speed, make every turn a braking turn and be sure to complete each one. Use the same flexion of ankles and knees to absorb the bump, but this time plant your pole and pivot both skis at the top of the bump. Slide down the back side, extending your legs into the trough to prepare for the next turn. Work your way down the slope, turning on the top of each mogul, and aim to stay close to the fall line. This technique works well, even on hard and icy bumps. The top of the bump, where you are setting the edge, accumulates the most snow and is usually softer than the sides where snow has been scraped off.

Fig 65(c) Extend skis into the trough.

Fig 65(d) A relaxed, anticipated stance prepares you for the following turn.

ANTICIPATION

The term 'anticipation' was coined by the French skier, Georges Joubert. Anticipation describes the position of your upper body as you face towards the inside of a turn prior to its initiation. It's a positive position achieved with a number of movements: a combination of pole plant and upper/lower body separation, with the dynamic movement of the upper body into the fall line. Anticipation creates a more powerful and efficient steering action on the skis, by ensuring that the upper body has anticipated lower body action.

Here's how it works. Plant your pole as you set your edge, and turn your body slightly in the direction you intend turning in. Now, as you rise to unweight the skis, crank your knees and feet around in the direction your upper body has already taken. In this way, anticipation prevents the torso from being left behind the action of your feet.

Anticipation is used to an increasing degree as slopes steepen. For the beginner, anticipation is simply keeping the eyes looking ahead, down the hill. An intermediate skier should anticipate by turning his chest and hands downhill as he pole plants, to create a more powerful, efficient steering action. On steeper slopes, an advanced skier plants his poles further back and faces more directly down the fall line to increase the effect of anticipation.

Note Planting the pole 'blocks' the upper body – keeping it facing downhill as the skier sets the edge. The result is a quiet, relaxed upper body with independent legs and feet absorbing the terrain and moving easily from side to side.

Figs 66(a)–(d) Anticipation.

Fig 66(a) Face downhill while traversing.

Fig 66(b) Looking in the direction of the next turn prior to turning.

Fig 66(c) On moderate terrain, plant the pole forward of your boot.

Fig 66(d) On steeper slopes, plant the pole further back to the side and face more directly down the fall line.

Fig 67   A quiet upper body. Skier Lisa Nicholas.

The Quiet Upper Body

Keeping your upper body quiet is part of anticipation. Your torso is your main mass. It takes less energy to keep a large mass moving in the same direction than to alter its path. This is momentum and it helps us to maintain balance as we descend – no bad thing!

A 'quiet' upper body is not a passive or rigid position. Quite the opposite, the torso is very active but it does something different from the lower body. Its energy is directed, contained in the skier's path. Stomach, back and buttocks all stretch and contract at every turn.

Use gravity and momentum, don't fight it; be loose and relaxed even when skiing hard and enjoy the ride – after all, that's why we ski.

Tip   Try moving your upper body towards the turn a little sooner than usual, just as you plant your pole. This makes for more dynamic skiing that is more in tune with gravity.

THE DYNAMIC PARALLEL (LONG RADIUS) TURN

Large turns should be both fluid and dynamic. The upper body carries momentum down the slope, while feet are pressed to the outside of the turn, steering and driving. Ride the ski, and use it as a tool.

Increasing speed is one way of making your turns more dynamic. The forces working on you and your equipment are intensified by speed. Practise the following exercise on a smooth, moderate slope, where you feel comfortable.

It may help to think of the opposite of dynamic: lethargic, passive, lacking in mental and physical alertness and activity. Dynamic skiing is as much a mental exercise as it is physical – don't be afraid to go for it!

A Long Radius Turn Exercise

Descend a moderate slope, clear

of bumps and obstacles, and practise initiating your turns by changing your weight onto the uphill ski and rolling it onto its inside edge. Changing your weight from downhill ski to uphill unweights you momentarily as you extend, making it easy to steer the new outside ski into the turn.

Tip   For more ski performance, press against the ball of your foot as you roll the ski on edge; this increases pressure on the ski's tip. As you complete the turn, feel the pressure closer to your heel, pressing on the ski's tail.

THE BANKED TURN

As you know, for a ski to function it must be placed on edge while turning. Skis can be edged with angulation or inclination (banking). Using angulation, knees are rolled towards and away from the slope to control edging, while the upper body remains relatively erect. A banked turn inclines the whole body to the inside of the turn and relies on momentum and centrifugal force to increase pressure on the skis' edges.

Banking is a relaxed method of turning and takes advantage of the efficiency of modern skis. Banking works well on smooth terrain.

Sufficient speed is necessary to initiate a banked turn. Plant your pole, then incline your whole body to the inside of the turn, pressing shins against the front of your boots to steer your skis. As with all turns, banked turns still require the outside ski to be weighted more than the inside one.

Tip   Smooth gullies are fun terrain for practising banked turns.

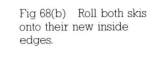

Fig 68(b)   Roll both skis onto their new inside edges.

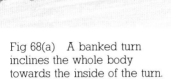

Fig 68(a)   A banked turn inclines the whole body towards the inside of the turn.

Figs 68(a)–(e)   The banked turn. A banked turn inclines the whole body to the inside of the turn and relies on momentum and centrifugal force to increase pressure on the skis' edges.

Fig 68(c)   Use edge angle and pressure to control the radius of the turn.

Fig 68(d)   Flex ankles and knees as you prepare to plant your pole.

Fig 68(e)   Pressure both skis, with more pressure on the outside ski.

ANGULATION

Angulation is active use of hips, knees and ankles to control edging of skis. Knees are rolled towards or away from the slope to affect the degree of edging, while the upper body remains relatively erect. Earlier in this book, sideslipping and traversing exercises were used to focus on controlling ski edges through the use of angulation. The following exercise focuses on feet and legs, and trains you to keep a quiet upper body moving in the right direction – down the hill and into the next turn.

Fig 69 Angulation. Kusan Staubli demonstrates.

An Angulation Exercise

Hold the ski poles across your chest as if carrying a tray of drinks. Aim to keep the poles horizontal while linking turns down an easy slope. Press shins against the front of your boots, towards the inside of each turn. Keep your upper body quiet and relaxed, and concentrate on using your knees to roll the skis on edge.

Fig 70(b)   Transfer pressure to the uphill ski at the start of each turn.

Fig 70(a)   Hold ski poles across your chest as if carrying a tray of drinks.

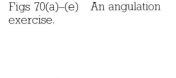

Figs 70(a)–(e)   An angulation exercise.

Figs 70(c) and (d)   Try to keep poles parallel to the snow.

Fig 70(e)   Keep your upper body quiet and relaxed.

CARVING

Skis have metal edges, a narrow waist and smooth flex for one reason – carving. The waist of a ski causes it to turn when placed on edge. Edging, without increasing pressure on the ski, results in long, drawn-out, carved turns. Pressing hard on those edges results in a sharper and more dynamic carved turn.

Carving is the most efficient means of turning. Watch a World Cup ski race. Look carefully as the racers turn. They are continually on edge, with their outside ski well away from their upper body and sharply inclined – all of their force is pressing on that edge to keep the ski carving. The winning skier will take the best line by skidding the least.

Become more aware of your edges by listening to your skis in the turn. Carved turns sound cleaner than skidded turns. This is especially noticeable on hard snow.

CARVING EXERCISES

Stepping on the Uphill Ski

Carved turns are the most efficient type of ski turn. To carve effectively, roll the uphill ski onto its inside edge and ride that edge right through the turn. Practise on a smooth intermediate slope.

Fig 71(a)

Figs 71(a)–(e)   A carving exercise: stepping onto the uphill ski. To initiate turning, step from the lower ski onto the uphill ski and roll the upper ski onto its inside edge. Ride that edge around the turn and repeat for the next turn.

Fig 71(b)

Fig 71(c)

Fig 71(e)

Fig 71(d)

Torro

The point of the torro exercise is to focus on keeping the upper body relaxed, facing downhill and advancing into each turn.

Hold poles forward, with your arms outstretched down the fall line of a gentle slope. Keep pole tips facing down the fall line as you descend, making regular turns. Stay loose at the hips and let your legs and feet do the turning.

Figs 72(a)–(c)   A torro exercise. As you ski a gentle slope, hold poles forward with arms outstretched down the fall line. Keep your upper body relaxed, facing downhill and advancing into each turn.

Fig 72(a)

Fig 72(b)

Fig 72(c)

Fig 73(a)

Fig 73(b)

The Crab Exercise

The crab exercise highlights edging and angulation. Face straight down the fall line of a smooth slope with skis opened into a large V. Descend, alternately flattening one ski and edging the other, moving across the slope on the edged ski. The upper body moves over the edged ski to increase edge pressure. The flattened ski brushes the snow as it moves sideways.

To emphasize the crab-like feeling, keep the torso – from hips to shoulders – facing straight down the fall line. Initially practise on a gentle slope, moving to steeper terrain as crab skill improves.

At higher speeds, the crab exercise becomes a power plough. The skier's movement is identical, but greater momentum increases edge pressure, emphasizing the carving action of the ski. Use a narrower wedge for power plough exercise.

Fig 73   A crab exercise (power plough). On a shallow slope, stand in the fall line with your skis opened into a large V. Alternately flatten one ski and edge the other. Move the upper body over the edged ski to increase pressure on the edge.

Fig 73(c)

SHORT RADIUS TURNS

Short radius turns require good co-ordination of all skills. The mechanics of shorter radius turns are the same as those for long radius turns, but swifter coordination and more power are necessary. The skier must exert a stronger pivoting action on the ski with a more aggressive style, especially on steeper slopes.

Rhythm is the first element that needs to be developed for dynamic short radius turns. Begin descending gentle slopes with rhythmic turns in the fall line, and progressively build to steeper terrain.

Tip Concentrate on just one element at a time to develop your timing: for example, the edge set or pole plant.

Put rhythm in your pole plant by counting a one/two beat as you touch the snow with poles, or concentrate on the edge set, by thinking left, right, left, etc. as you set that ski's edge.

Note A great deal of practice is needed to make consistent short radius turns. Practise on smooth, easy slopes until you begin to acquire consistent rhythm.

The Spiess Exercise

I once had a ski-school examiner named Craig Spiess – although he swore not to have invented this exercise, he was a master at making it look effortless.

The Spiess exercise focuses on the skill of pivoting and is designed to improve short radius turns. It also works on timing and coordination skills. You may not find the Spiess exercise easy at first, but persevering will pay off with improved turns.

Fig 74(a)

Fig 74(b)

Figs 74(a)–(e) The Spiess exercise. Stand directly in the fall line of a moderate slope and descend by hopping skis from inside edge to inside edge. Keep poles to the side and out of the way.

Fig

Fig 74(d)

Fig 74(e)

Fig 75(a)   Flex ankles as you plant your pole.

Figs 75(a)–(d)   The short radius turn using up-unweighting. A continuously anticipated position, with quiet upper body facing down the fall line, is the most agile one; legs are displaced from side to side with a strong pivoting action.

Fig 75(b)   Extend to lighten skis and pivot both feet.

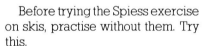

Before trying the Spiess exercise on skis, practise without them. Try this.

Standing in place, hop up and down, rotating your feet left to right each hop. Face a full-length mirror while doing the exercise, and make sure that the foot-pivoting action takes place from below the hip, while the upper body remains facing forwards. Keep your hands up and out to the side, as if holding ski poles.

On snow, stand directly in the fall line of a moderate slope and descend by hopping skis from inside edge to inside edge. Don't let the skis slide. Set the edge firmly every time. Do six of these and you are doing well, sixty and you're a hero!

Powerful flexion and extension are required to change direction. Keep your poles to the side and out of the way. Be light on your feet and pivot both skis as they come clear of the snow. Remember, extension begins at the ankle!

Fig 75(c)   Face down the fall line displacing feet from side to side with a strong pivoting action.

Fig 75(d)   Flex ankles and knees in preparation for the following turn.

Fig 76(a)

Fig 76(b)

Fig 76(c)

DOWN-UNWEIGHTING

Until now you have used up-unweighting as the basic means of unweighting skis to initiate turns. Down-unweighting works on the same principle as up-unweighting, but results from a rapid downward motion and is more effective for quick turns.

The correct way to down-unweight is to simultaneously drop hips and flex ankles and knees forwards. It is the speed of the motion, not how far you move, that is important. Generally, down-unweighting is used for very rapid changes of direction and up-unweighting when you have more time. Get out the bathroom scales again and try flexing your ankles rapidly; the scales will show a momentary drop in weight. In a down-unweighted turn, this motion coincides with steering your skis.

The Hockey Stop

A hockey turn or stop is an abrupt change of direction across the fall line using down-unweighting. The skier's rapid 'sinking down' motion briefly unweights skis, enabling the feet to pivot easily.

Advanced skiers benefit from using this manoeuvre to train for short radius turns and powder snow.

During a hockey stop, both feet are steered simultaneously.

A Hockey Stop Exercise

(Or, how to spray friends with snow.) Begin with skis in the fall line and descend straight down a moderate slope, standing tall on your skis. Now bring yourself to an abrupt halt by sinking down with a rapid movement, and simultaneously pivot your feet (with some force) across the fall line.

Figs 76(a)–(f) The Hockey Stop. Descend straight down a moderate slope, standing tall on your skis. Bring yourself to an abrupt halt by sinking down with a rapid movement, and simultaneously pivot your feet across the fall line.

Fig 76(d)

Fig 76(e)

Fig 76(f)

THE SHORT RADIUS TURN (Using Down-Unweighting)

Rapid and sure short radius turns are the mark of the advanced skier. A continuously anticipated position, with quiet upper body facing down the fall line, is the most agile one; legs are displaced from side to side, similarly to a pendulum. Imagine a cat jumping from rock to rock: quick and agile, but also relaxed, ready for anything. That's how to ski!

Short radius turns are aggressive, but that doesn't mean that you should be tense. Excessive movement of the upper body and arms is a common fault when trying to ski aggressively – relax. Use the rebound effect of setting the edge to bounce from turn to turn.

Down-unweighting is the most effective means of lightening skis during rapid turning.

Figs 77(a)–(d) The short radius turn using down-unweighting. Sometimes a picture is worth a thousand words. Study this sequence very carefully; Kusan is demonstrating flawless technique. Notice in photo (c) how the uphill ski becomes the outside ski in the turn.

Fig 77(a)

Fig 77(b)

Fig 77(c)

Fig 77(d)

Skier Rolf Liechti

5 Challenges

ADVANCED MOGULS

Almost every ski resort has its show-boat run, usually beneath a chairlift, where hot skiers can be spied flying through Volkswagen-sized moguls. Perhaps you'll never ski Exhibition in Sun Valley, Idaho, or Al's Run at Taos, New Mexico, but you can learn the technique. The secret to skiing bumps at speed is to learn something called a terrain un-weighted turn.

Terrain Unweighting

Terrain unweighting is a rather technical term for letting the bumps do the work. It's not as complicated as it sounds – the skier simply takes advantage of changes in terrain to turn where skis feel lightest, at the crest of the rise. Terrain unweighting refines the skills you worked on when first learning to absorb uneven terrain.

Flexion and extension are vital again, but this time skis are drawn beneath you to unweight between turns, and pressed to the outside of the turn to carve. Check for upper-body position by keeping your belly button pointing downhill.

To familiarize yourself with the feeling, find a smooth, rolling slope. Descend in big, wide turns, changing edges where your skis feel light, at the crest of each roll. Then head into some long, round moguls on a moderate (not too steep) slope. Take it easy at first; use a relaxed, athletic position.

Work towards shortening up your turns, letting momentum carry you into the rise of the bump, and turn where your skis feel light. You don't have to collapse like an accordian; flex strongly at the ankles to absorb the bumps.

The biggest and most common problem that skiers have with bumps isn't technique, but intimidation – fear gets in the way. Work on your short radius turns and practise terrain unweighting to develop confidence.

To improve short radius turning technique and develop rhythm, in preparation for moguls, practise short radius turns on smooth groomed slopes, in a cat track for example. Face straight down the hill with your hands in view, keeping the upper body quiet.

Absorption

Skiing smoothly through moguls means absorbing them. Traversing across bumps develops your ability to absorb bumps and extend in the troughs. Practise skiing moguls by connecting round parallel turns with traverses through the bumps.

A common mistake in moguls is to absorb the first few bumps, then to stay low and blocked, gathering speed.

Prevention is the best solution. Start slow and build rhythm. Stay loose, pressing your skis into the troughs. Complete each turn to keep your speed under control.

Fig 78   Terrain unweighting.

Figs 79(a)–(c)   Traversing in moguls – absorption.

Fig 79(a)

Fig 79(b)

Fig 79(c)

Line

Top mogul skiers ski directly in the fall line, turning continuously. To maintain their line they look directly down the slope. In the following photograph, notice how US Free-style Ski Team member Liz Mcintyre is carving a turn along the side of the bump, not straight over the top. This permits her to ski a more direct line in huge moguls.

Fig 80   US Freestyle Ski Team member Liz Mcintyre carving a turn along the side of a bump.

Fig 81(a)

Figs 81(a)–(d) Pole plant in moguls. Former World Cup mogul competitor, Lisa Nicholas, demonstrates. Notice her easy line through the bumps.

Fig 81(b)

Pole Plant

Rhythm is the key to skiing bumps, as it is to much of skiing. The pole plant provides the beat to keep rhythm with. The idea is to keep your rhythm going, no matter what the terrain throws up at you.

Most mogul skiers use a pole 5cm (2in) or so shorter than average. Shorter poles don't get hung up on the bumps while descending at speed.

A good friend of mine, Henrik Oscarsson (ranked number three in World Cup mogul competition in 1986), continually practised his pole plant and was rarely without poles even when walking in the hills. That's how important it is.

Fig 81(c)

Fig 81(d)

Fig 83(a)

Fig 82   Using a mogul to help turning.

Anticipation

In advanced mogul technique, the upper body faces continually down the fall line. This anticipated position results in a quiet, relaxed upper body with independent legs and feet absorbing the terrain and moving easily from side to side. The upper body follows a more direct path than the skis do.

Fig 83(b)

Figs 83(a) and (b)   Anticipation in moguls. Rolf Liechti demonstrates.

Figs 84(a)–(e)   Mogul skiing. In this side view, flexion and extension are very apparent as Rolf absorbs the crest of each bump and extends into the troughs.

Fig 84(a)   Use terrain unweighting to absorb the mogul.

Fig 84(b)   Extend into the trough.

Figs 84(c),(d) and (e)   Deep flexion is necessary in large moguls.

(d)

(e)

Fig 85   Powder bumps.

JUMPING

Apart from being a lot of fun, jumping helps build courage and confidence. Start with little jumps while descending a gentle slope in the fall line. For extra distance and altitude, progress to a gentle roll, and practise extending just before the top of the roll.

A long jump on alpine skis is called a *gelandesprung*. To jump flex your ankles and knees, then extend rapidly springing upwards and forwards off the snow. To land easily, keep your hands forward and extend your legs before touchdown, flexing ankles and knees on landing to absorb the shock.

Gradually increase the length of your jumps by climbing further up the hill; increase height by springing more on take-off. For extra distance, tuck your knees up near your chest in the air, extending your legs again for landing.

Intermediates should feel comfortable gliding a couple of ski lengths through the air, and advanced skiers much further. For even greater distance, use a slope with an easy in-run, a landing hill of thirty to forty per cent, and a safe transition to flat for an out-run; medium-hard snow. Gradually build courage by practising jumping at slow speeds, and work on extending more on take-off.

Note Jumping need not be a high-energy activity; being able to get skis easily off the ground is the mark of a smooth skier.

Fig 86   A *gelandesprung*.

Fig 87   Landing.

The Aerial Turn

An aerial turn is a turn made in the air between bumps. Successful aerial turns are jumps coordinating swift movements with precise timing.

Find a section of smooth, round moguls to train in. Study the terrain before jumping, practise the line without taking air during the first few runs. When you have more experience, you'll be able to jump spontaneously.

Take air by extending from an edge set near the crest of the mogul. Tuck your skis beneath you, turning them in the air, and land on the inside edge of your outside (downhill) ski. Keep both hands up and forward for balance.

For smooth landings, touch down on the downhill side of the next bump (preferably a long, round mogul leading into a good line). Experienced bump skiers sometimes land two or more moguls further down the slope.

Henrik told me that landing with skis on edge is the key to being able to continue turning in the fall line. The skis' rebound effect propels you into the next turn.

With practice, perhaps you'll even start throwing helicopters and other aerial manoeuvres such as cossacks, daffies and twisters. For now, find yourself a group of keen mogul skiers and get out there and ski bumps, as often and for as long as possible – there's no other way. It's hard work, but think how much fun it will be!

Fig 88(e)   Extend legs for landing.

Fig 88(f)   Touch down on the downhill side of the next bump.

Fig 88(g)   Land with skis on edge to finish the turn.

Fig 88(c)

Fig 88(b)–(d)   Tuck skis
beneath you, turning them in
the air.

Fig 88(d)

Figs 88(a)–(g)   An aerial turn.

Fig 88(a)   Extend from an
edge set near the crest of a
mogul.

Fig 89 'Spread eagle', during a World Cup mogul competition.

MOGUL EQUIPMENT

Skis

Mogul skiing demands quick-turning, sturdy skis with sharp edges (the snow in the troughs can be very hard). Slalom racing skis are used by most mogul competitors. Most men use a ski around 200cm (79in) and women generally use 190cm (75in).

A smaller ski will be quicker to turn, but less smooth. Shorter lengths are designed for lighter skiers, and are more likely to break if used by heavier skiers. Don't use skis with metal layers for mogul skiing; they are more likely to bend or delaminate.

If you plan to do much mogul skiing, check the ski's warranty before you buy; some manufacturers will not replace skis that have been damaged because of skiing in moguls.

Tune your skis with a little extra bevel in the tip for easier turn initiation in the bumps. Keep them sharp!

Boots

Precise edge control and sensitive snow feel are needed for maximum performance in moguls. Boots that offer this kind of performance are stiffer than others and may give your shins a bruising if your technique is more bash than finesse.

Build up speed as your skill improves, not before.

EXTREME SKIING

This term is in vogue just now. In Europe it usually means that to fall is certain death. European extreme skiers acquire their reputation by making first descents of famous peaks. To increase the degree of difficulty (and publicity), skiers put together 'enchainments', skiing two or three 60- to 65-degree slopes in a day. Pierre Tardivel, perhaps the world's finest extreme skier, has over three dozen first descents or premiers on some of the most radical peaks in the Alps.

Acccording to Tardivel (quoted in *Powder Magazine* interview, vol. 20 no. 2), ice is the biggest hazard, especially on north faces, where it may be covered by a layer of powder snow. He feels that climbing a slope before skiing it is the only way to properly check the slope's conditions. He also stresses that the potentially lethal dangers in high mountains can never be neglected.

In the United States, 'extreme skiing' is mostly about skiing steep, challenging lines, where it is necessary to jump rocks and other obstacles – not about dying. A number of skiers have managed to carve out a niche for themselves in this field, skiing radical slopes for the cameras. It's easy to forget in the midst of publicity that these skiers are extremely talented professionals, with a wealth of experience behind them. Many of them were downhill racers in their previous incarnation, and are comfortable skiing at speeds in excess of 120kph (75mph).

I have been lucky enough to ski with a few of them: Scott Schmidt, Tom Day, John Egan and Glen Plake (the guy in the ads with the 'hawk'

Fig 90 Glen Plake 'mule kicks' into the sunset.

haircut). In every case I found them reasoning individuals, intently interested in safety and *very* hot skiers. To try to emulate their example without their experience and training is potentially deadly.

For jumping cliffs, they use long skis, 210 to 220cm (83 to 87in). The length softens the impact and makes control possible after landing a jump from great height. (The record is something like 50 metres (164ft!)

If you decide that cliff jumping is for you, practise air by beginning with small drops. The landing hill is the most critical factor; it should be steep, to reduce impact and have a clear run-out. Deep powder greatly increases the safety of a height – be certain before jumping that no rocks or trees are hidden by the snow.

STEEPS

Skiing steeps requires more than courage. The most vital ingredient for successful steep descents is speed control.

Speed control comes from the edge set, and here's the irony. A strong edge set requires a firm commitment to the downhill ski, the one that fear pulls you away from. If you are finding it hard to commit your weight to the downhill ski, concentrate instead on keeping your upper body away from the slope and down the fall line. It is scary at first, but doing this automatically helps you to weight the downhill ski with a firm edge set.

Quick edge sets and tight short radius turns work well on ordinarily steep slopes of thirty to forty degrees or so. The technique used to control speed on steep steeps (the limit is around sixty degrees) is the pedal turn. As the name suggests, this turn works with a pedal action. This action allows the skier to turn in the air and avoid accelerating down the fall line.

To initiate the pedal turn, push off very hard with the uphill ski to get clear of the snow, and pivot your skis in the air. Land on the new downhill ski, with skis parallel

Fig 92   Lisa Nicholas pedal turning in a steep couloir.

across the fall line, and set edges to control speed. Remember, keep your upper body directed towards the valley.

Don't jump too high, just enough to clear the snow. If necessary, this technique permits you to come to a complete stop every turn, but a rhythmic descent is preferable.

A solid pole plant helps to keep balance and rhythm. The steeper the terrain, the further back and to the side the pole must be planted to maintain an anticipated position (essential for linking turns on the steep).

Practise skiing steeps on short pitches, where a fall will not be hazardous to your health.

Fig 91   Extreme skiing. The skier is Kusan Staubli.

Equipment

The gear required to conquer steeps is not specialized. Skis must be well prepared; this is no time to catch an edge or slip on an icy patch, tuned skis provide an extra measure of security. Slightly longer poles extend your reach.

Fear

Skiing steeps is a mental game, and the right frame of mind can be the biggest obstacle. Fear is a natural element, it keeps you honest. Use its by-products, energy and adrenalin, to focus on the moment. Total concentration is the key to control.

Steep couloirs, ice and deep snow need to be approached with respect and patience. Don't scare yourself or try to take on too much too soon. The key to conquering new challenges is to build up to these conditions slowly, gaining experience over time.

SPEED

Beyond the obvious rush of high speeds, developing the ability to ski with speed does much to improve your skiing in general.

If you are a serious speedster, keen to try out downhill and speed courses, consider signing up for a race clinic. Racing clinics are available to both adults and children, and are the best way to learn about downhill or speed racing technique in a safe environment.

An increasing number of resorts have permanent speed courses available to the public. If you merely want a taste of the excitement, check with a resort's ski school or information office for speed courses availability. Usually, a few runs through the speed trap and some

Fig 93   The tuck. The position for maximum speed.

helpful pointers from a pro are available to the keen novice for a moderate fee.

At the top level of the sport of speed skiing, skiers wear special aerodynamic equipment: slippery skin suits with foam 'fins' behind the legs, aerodynamic helmets and curved poles. Skis that are 240cm (95in) provide stability at 200kph (125mph).

Skiing at Speed

So you want to go fast without taking to a speed course with a pair of 240s and a skin-tight suit.

Long cruising runs, made for speed, exist in most ski resorts and are not hard to find. However, be aware of what rules apply to them. Not all resorts encourage speed. In general, US resorts are the most uptight about fast skiing – multiple lawsuits have made them that way. In Canada, most resorts recognize that wide, open runs are made for speed, and fast skiing is generally permitted away from beginner slopes. In Europe, 'ski at your own risk' is a way of life, and there are

few restrictions on fast skiers.

Speeding on cruising runs absent of moguls and sudden drop-offs can appear deceptively simple, but speed tolerates few mistakes. A minor lapse in control, easily regained in normal circumstances, can mean a major wipe-out at high speeds.

Skiing effectively at high speeds requires a few modifications in style. Save the short, sharp turns for short, sharp runs. Aim for fewer, but larger, radius turns and don't fight the terrain.

Speed Equipment

Specialized 'skin' suits are not essential to enjoy fast skiing, but longer skis are a must. (They don't have to be 220cm (87in) downhill boards – 205s (81in) will do to start, but 210s (83in) or 215s (85in) are even better). Long skis are stable and made for speed. The latest racing skis, even downhill models, are not hard to turn.

Make sure that your bindings are properly adjusted and lubricated to absorb shock; a premature re-

Fig 94   Speed racing equipment. A slippery speed suit, aerodynamic helmet, foam 'fins' behind legs, and curved poles. 240cm (95in) long skis for stability at 200kph (125mph).

lease can be more dangerous than no release at all. Bindings with heavier springs are recommended for safety.

Boots for speed must fit well, offer stiff lateral support and flex smoothly.

Stance

Speed requires a wider stance; let your skis spread apart 15–20cm (7–9in). Moving your feet further apart not only provides greater balance and comfort but, more importantly, allows you to unweight and shift from edge to edge in the turn without lifting a ski. This is a quicker, smoother edge transfer.

Edge Control for Carved Turns

Carved turns and edge control are

what speed is all about. Edge control is easy to lose at high speeds. The best way to maintain edge control and ski through a turn without skidding is to keep all of your weight on the inside edge of the outside ski. Then, when it's time to turn, without letting your skis ride flat on the snow, quickly shift your weight onto the inside edge of the new outside ski with a rolling action. Keep the edge hold happening all through the turn, and maintain a quiet upper body with your hands out in front. Use poles for rhythm, not force; in a high-speed turn you need only graze the snow with your pole to time the edge transfer.

The best way to develop carving ability is to start slowly. Practise on a smooth, wide slope, making long, slow traverses back and forth. Hold the downhill ski angled into the hill the whole time. Join the traverses with round cruising turns, carving the turns with the inside edge of the outside ski and shifting weight with the rolling motion as described above. Develop the feeling for car-

Fig 95   Australian downhill racer, Steven Lee, carving a turn at 120kph (75mph).

ving before working on it at high speeds.

Cautionary note   Skiing with speed requires great use of reflexes and concentration. Stay both focused ahead and thinking ahead. The downside of speed is that falls can be painful and damaging. Experiment with speed only on the appropriate slope, well away from slower skiers.

Fig 96   Fast is fun. (Speed skier's bumper sticker.)

6 Powder, Ice and Crust

POWDER

Deep powder snow is an expert skier's dream. The technique is graceful, elegant and (with experience) almost effortless. Powder supports you, slows you and helps you to turn. Very deep snow gives the skier a sensation of floating that any other sport would find hard to match.

Except for a modification in technique, powder skiing uses the same fundamental skills as skiing on hard snow.

The Essentials

1. Weight the skis evenly. Because your skis are actually floating in the snow, each ski must receive equal pressure. Keep your feet close together; even squeeze them together so that they act as one. Fore and aft weight placement should also be neutral, over the centre of your feet (perhaps slightly back, over your heels, for stiffer skis, but don't lean backwards).

2. Keep your speed up. A certain amount of speed is needed to gain enough momentum for the skis to begin to float. Don't hold back.

3. Ski in the fall line. The fall line offers the least resistance and is the easiest direction to ski powder in. Fall line skiing places you in an anticipated position; the upper body can stay quiet and let the feet and legs work rhythmically from side to side. Control speed with the radius of your turns.

4. Keep your hands forward. Letting a hand fall back twists your upper body away from its anticipated position, making it difficult to stay in the fall line.

5. Ski rhythmically, flexing and extending fully. Rhythm keeps you floating from one turn to the next. Motion keeps you stable. No one turn is an end in itself, all turns link together in a flow of energy down the mountain.

Skier Rolf Liechti.

Fig 97   Powder.

Powder Practice

Find a smooth, shallow, to moderate slope, ideally with around 30cm (12in) of fresh, light snow. Stay well clear of rocks and trees.

Begin your first attempts by gliding straight down a shallow slope. Try alternately weighting each foot; your skis will probably take on a life of their own and go off in every direction.

Next descend the same slope, keeping weight equally distributed over both skis – I find that squeezing the feet together helps. This time your skis will both track in the same direction.

Rhythm, is the key to successful powder turns. A solid pole plant, combined with rhythmic flexion and extension, is needed. Descend again, in a straight run, planting poles and bouncing rhythmically with each pole plant.

The next step is to combine rhythmic bouncing with turning your feet. Make regular turns in the fall line by bouncing off both feet equally and landing on both equally, edging both skis at exactly the same time. Imagine that your skis are one platform.

The powder turn is not a sharp, abrupt manoeuvre. Each turn contains a wind-up and a release of energy, which powers you into the next turn. A common mistake is to rush. Slow down your actions and feel what's happening. This is how rhythm is developed.

Adapt your technique to the snow and terrain.

If the snow is very heavy, use 'projection' to power yourself through. Projection means to use your upper body, notably your arms, to help you to unweight.

In light, easy snow on moderate slopes, use avalement or down-unweighting to turn (see page 70).

Fig 98(a)

Figs 98(a)–(g)   Powder skiing. Rolf Liechti demonstrates.

Fig 98(b)

Fig 98(c)

Fig 98(d)

POWDER TIPS

1. Imagine your skis as a single platform.
2. Weight both skis equally.
3. Don't rush your turns.
4. Be rhythmic from one turn to the next.

Fig 98(f)

Fig 98(e)

Fig 98(g)

89

Fig 99   Skis leave pretty tracks in powder snow.

Powder Equipment

For powder skiing, some skiers prefer longer poles and a softer ski, such as a soft slalom model.

A few ski manufacturers make special wide soft powder skis. These may be useful if powder is the only condition that you are likely to experience in a day – when helicopter skiing for example. Real life, though, often means skiing powder in the morning and bumps in the afternoon; soft-flexing, slalom-type skis are much more versatile.

If, like me, you enjoy making high-speed, large radius turns in powder and carving up the whole slope, you may find that longer giant slalom-type skis suit you better.

Note   Powder slows you down. The correct wax is important to make skis slide and turn easily, especially in wet, fresh snow and very cold conditions.

CRUD

The sun can quickly turn even the best snow into crud, especially in spring. Being in good aerobic condition is beneficial when learning to ski difficult snow. Warm up properly to prevent injury. Abdominal muscle strength in particular is a great advantage in tough snow conditions.

It is easy to exhaust yourself when learning to ski heavy snow. Take breaks often; you will learn faster when rested and relaxed.

Jump Turns

In heavy crud, when normal turns feel like wading through wet concrete, use jump turns to clear the snow and pivot skis in the air. Masters of this technique can clear the snow from their skis in mid-air.

Jump turns are an effective way of skiing junk snow, but only while your stamina holds out. Jump turns are a tough work-out, especially on abdominal muscles.

The following exercise is similar to the Spiess exercise in chapter 4, but requires extra effort to clear skis of heavy snow.

Face directly down the hill, with skis across the slope. Set the uphill edges of both skis; this forms a platform to turn from. Plant your poles and raise your outside shoulder or arm for momentum. Now suck up your legs and crank the skis around to land with them parallel in the new direction. Land on both skis at the same time.

Figs 100(a)–(d) Jump turns. Lisa
Nicholas demonstrates.

Fig 100(a) Set the uphill
edges of both skis, forming a
platform.

Fig 100(b) Plant pole and
extend off the uphill ski, raising
outside shoulder or arm for
added momentum in heavy
snow.

Fig 100(c) Pivot skis in the air.

Fig 100(d) Land on both skis
at the same time.

91

Fig 101(a)

Fig 101(b)

Figs 101(a)–(f) Slush. With strong technique, even deep and slushy snow such as these melted sun cups can be skied with elegance and style. Kusan Staubli demonstrates.

Fig 101(c)

BREAKABLE CRUST

Crust is formed by wind or sun and can vary in thickness from a thin glaze, easily sliced through, to thick slabs, able to support a skier's weight. Crust that supports you only *some* of the time is the most difficult to ski and demands extra finesse. **Note** The risk of avalanche is always greatest when crust begins to break. This condition should be avoided if at all possible.

Fig 102 Rolf uses a high-speed jump turn to ski breakable crust – soft snow that refroze.

Fig 101(d)

Fig 101(e)

Fig 101(f)

93

Sometimes crust forms a meringue-like surface that supports your weight but grabs edges and breaks with too much pressure. The best technique for this form of crust is the stem turn.

The Stem Turn

A stem turn allows you to stay very light on your skis and to avoid breaking crust. Stem turns also work well for other difficult conditions and when carrying a heavy pack. Stem turning is the easy way to ski catchy snow.

Flex very low and open your outside ski into a wedge. Touch your pole to signal rising, and transfer your weight onto the outside ski. Stand tall on your outside ski and ride it around the turn. Actively flex both ankles to finish the turn and create a platform from which to rise into the next turn.

Fig 103(d)

Fig 103(e)

Fig 103(g)

Fig 103(f)

Fig 103(a)

Fig 103(b)

Fig 103(c)

Figs 103(a)–(g) The stem turn. A stem turn allows you to stay very light on your skis and avoid breaking crust. Kusan Staubli demonstrates.

Avalanche!

The greatest fear of most off-piste skiers is (or should be) to be caught in an avalance. More skiers are becoming adept at skiing in deep snow, and the competition for first tracks increases. This keenness, combined with lack of awareness, leads to many accidents. Take nothing for granted and don't ski off piste without the knowledge to back you. Skiing off piste with a qualified guide is strongly recommended.

Knowledge is your best protection. Take a course in mountain safety if you have the opportunity. A number of books on the subject are available too. *Avalance Awareness* by Martin Epp and Stephen Lee is recommended.

Fig 104   Apprentice guide, Hans Solmssen, studying layers in the snow pack, evaluating the risk before skiing the slope.

Fig 105   Hans using a magnifying glass to look for hoar-frost crystals – the most dangerous layer.

Fig 106   Wind deposits loose snow on leeward slopes. Even a small snowfall can lead to sizeable deposits and dangerous snow slabs if the wind is strong.

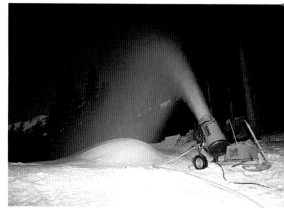

Fig 108   A snow gun. These machines transform water into snow to make skiing possible when natural snowfall is light.

ICE

I grew up skiing on ice in eastern Canada. We called it snow most of the time, but what came out of those snow guns in the early years of the technology was definitely closer to a skating rink than the powder snow I was later to encounter. Good technique was needed to avoid finishing a day's skiing black and blue.

These days, snow guns pump out more snow than ever and snow-grooming equipment has never been more sophisticated, but ice still exists. Luckily, skis have never been better, and if you keep them well tuned, even very hard snow is fun to ski.

Fig 109   A snow-grooming machine. Working the night shift to provide good conditions for the morning – *merci*! thank you!

Fig 107   A skier started this slab avalanche on a north-facing slope. The slab was created by wind; note that the slope is convex halfway down. Convex slopes are more dangerous because the snow is under tension. The accident was fatal – learn from others' mistakes.

Fig 110   Skiing on ice. Keep your upper body balanced over the outside ski. Use angulation, not banking. Kusan demonstrates on frozen spring snow.

Ice Technique

The single most important factor when skiing ice is to be light on your feet, to ski more loosely. Put your skis out there on edge, balance over the outside ski, but don't rely on them to grip every turn. When your edges grip, the result will be a carved turn; when they don't, you won't be thrown off balance.

Note the following points.

1.   Pay attention to your line; even on extremely icy slopes there is usually snow on the crests of moguls. Use the patches of snow to set your edges and control speed.

2.   Widen your stance slightly; this gives more stability if edges fail to grip.
3.   Have skis always on edge, carving all the way through each turn, never accelerating flat on the snow.
4.   Pressure the middle of the outside ski, not the tip or tail.
5.   Never lean into the hill; you'll be off your edges and onto your newly bruised hip faster than greased lightning! Keep your upper body balanced over the outside ski. Use *angulation* not banking.
6.   Keep turning. Even though edges may not grip well every turn, the less time you spend on edge, the less chance you have of slipping.

7.   Minimal unweighting is needed on ice; edge gradually to avoid chattering skis. Be sensitive to snow contact.
8.   Ski smoothly on ice, as you would drive a car.

Note   If you encounter pure water ice (the hardest kind – with no snow content), relax and steer your skis to the next patch of snow to edge and slow down. At the edge of even the iciest trails, there is usually a berm of snow piled up. The difference between the skier who flashes by and the one struggling may be that the speedy skier has learned to read the surface better.

Drifting over glare patches and edging on the grippier parts comes with experience.

Skiing ice is a subtle art. Mistakes can result in nasty bruising – all the more reason for caution at first.

Equipment for Ice

The right equipment is a big advantage on slippery slopes.

Skis A good racing ski is ideal for icy slopes; having recently sharpened edges is equally important. To expect to ski 'boilerplate' (the name given to very icy snow in eastern North America – a region notorious for hard conditions) on untuned, dull skis would be a big mistake. In extreme conditions, use a pocket hone and touch-up file every day. World Cup racers go so far as to sharpen their slalom skis to a very acute angle: completely flat on the base with an edge angle of 87 degrees. Skis this sharp are practically impossible for the uninitiated to ski on, but keep racers on course in bulletproof conditions (as you can see, there is no lack of terms for describing icy snow!).

Boots Precision-fitting boots are very important on ice. Most racers prefer stiff, overlap entry boots that offer quick response time and improve edge control. They are essential for really attacking icy slopes.

Note Boots must match your strength and ability: don't buy slalom racing machines if you are not strong enough to flex them – a softer version would suit better.

Poles Ice does not require special poles, but I prefer sharp-tipped ones.

SKIING BEYOND AREA BOUNDARIES

Skiing away from controlled slopes is a great source of freedom and adventure. For me, it is a principal reason why I ski full time.

Sometimes the reward for hiking to 'off-piste' terrain is the lightest and easiest cotton-wool powder, or perfect spring snow, at other times the challenge is harder, harsh conditions such as ice, strong winds or crud. Dealing with the elements is one of the great joys of skiing. With a positive attitude, and a determination to have fun, ice, breakable crust, steep slopes and the rest can produce as many ear-to-ear grins as powder will.

Rules of the Road

The freedom to ski outside ski-area boundaries comes with responsibility. Risk is increased away from controlled slopes. If you don't understand the risks involved, you should not be there. It's up to you, or your guide, to decide if a slope is safe. Take the responsibility seriously, and at all times be aware of how your actions affect others.

Here are a few 'rules of the road', to put you on the right track.

1. Pay attention to avalanche warnings. They're posted for your safety. Don't be afraid to ask the local ski patrol for advice; they'll be happy to help.
2. Learn about avalanches, especially the effects of steepness and temperature on the snowpack. The more you know, the greater your respect will be for the dangers involved.
3. Do not ski out of bounds during periods of bad visibility, unless you know the run in your sleep.
4. Be aware of hidden crevasses on glaciers.
5. Starting and finishing early provides an extra measure of security. Stay within bounds late in the day. If an accident should occur, search and rescue is much more complicated after dark. Don't forget, nightfall arrives early in midwinter, when it can be dark at 4.30 p.m.
6. Wear an avalanche beeper.

Fig 111   Be aware of crevasses! These crevasses are easy to see, but others may be hidden. The skier is Glen Plake.

7 Local Knowledge

Vacation time is precious. This chapter is about making the most of your ski time, with useful advice on where and when to ski to avoid crowds and find the best snow.

AVOIDING CROWDS

Skiing is a very popular sport, and if you are unlucky enough to hit the wrong lift on the wrong day, you can find yourself wasting hours in lift queues. The secret to avoiding crowds is advance planning.

1.   Ski off peak.

(a)   Ski in January. January is low season in most ski resorts. Okay, the days are shorter and temperatures generally lower (especially in North America) than at other times, but the snow can be the best of the year and crowds are light. Wear warm clothing, and enjoy.

(b)   Ski in the spring. In springtime, resorts often have the best snow cover and the fewest skiers. While others are cleaning golf clubs and restringing tennis racquets, you could be skiing deserted slopes. Most resorts close in the spring because of lack of skiers, not lack of snow.

(c)   Avoid school-holiday periods if you can. These are the busiest periods at most resorts.

2.   If you must ski during holiday periods, be at the lift early to keep ahead of the crowd. If the lift opens at 8.30 a.m., being there at 8.25 instead of 9.05 will make a huge difference to your day.

3.   Lunch early. If you were able to get off to that early start, you should be ready for a break just as the late-morning crowds are filling the slopes. Lunching early also means fresher food and faster service! The other advantage of an early lunch is that by the time most people are queuing for theirs, you'll be back on the slopes.

4.   Ski late. If you have the energy, stay up until the last run. This can be especially pleasant at resorts

Fig 112   Plan a trip to a refuge for lunch! The Cabane Mont Fort in Verbier.

with summit restaurants. You can sip hot chocolate and watch the sun set while the slopes clear, then ski empty pistes home. (Make sure that you are warmly dressed.)

Note Beginning skiers must allow enough time to get down before the ski patrol 'sweeps' the slopes!

DISCOVERY

Skiing a new resort can be a big time waster. It's fun to explore new terrain, but you don't want to be skiing crud while, unknown to you, others are carving up the best snow of the year!

Hiring a guide is a sure way to locate the best skiing. Guides know which slopes to ski in the morning, which in the afternoon, and the best place to lunch, etc. Some resorts (especially in the States) employ hosts and hostesses, available for free tours of the area. Take advantage!

Although a guide is one way to get on the fast track, exploring a resort with friends can be as much fun, if you know where to start looking.

Midwinter

In midwinter (December to February), the sun is low in the sky and has less effect on snow conditions than it does in the spring. If there is fresh snow, stay on east- and south-facing slopes in the morning and enjoy the sunshine. If the snow is old, dress warmly and head straight to north-facing slopes for the best conditions.

Spring

Spring conditions are the most variable due to extreme changes in temperature and the strength of the sun. A thaw–freeze cycle (hot days

Fig 113   Perfect spring snow is easy to ski! The skier is Kusan Staubli.

followed by cold nights) produces spring snow – often called corn snow because of its consistency. During the day the snow melts and smooths out, and at night it refreezes to form a shell-like finish.

Good, smooth spring snow is a fantastic surface to ski on, and better than any prepared piste. Imagine a whole mountain covered in a smooth finish, with just the right texture for edging – spring snow at its best.

Timing is everything with spring snow. Begin the day on east-facing slopes and follow the sun as it comes around, finishing on west-facing slopes. (**Note**: If you are skiing early in spring, there may still be powder on north-facing slopes. In this case, rise early to ski the powder before following the sun through the spring snow.)

Plan to arrive at the top of spring snow slopes with the sun, or just before and wait a few minutes for the slope to soften. Don't tarry; later in the day the same surface may start to break and be liable to avalanche.

Even if the crust is not breaking, skiing spring snow too late in the day will spoil the surface for future visits. Move to another slope if your skis begin to leave tracks in the snow.

Remember: The rule for spring snow is to stop skiing a slope when your skis begin to mark the snow. In this way, excellent skiing will last as long as the weather holds. If you leave tracks, these will freeze during the night and be terrible to ski over until the next snowfall.

Late Spring

Late in the season, snow conditions are very unpredictable. There may

Fig 114   Foggy below, perfect conditions above!

be great snow everywhere, but chances are that if it has not been freezing at night in the village, south-facing slopes will have rotten snow and the best skiing will be found on northern exposures.

Important note Be especially cautious if the previous night has been warm. Avalanches in spring snow are most common following warmer nights when the crust re-freezes for only a short period of time, perhaps two hours or less. In these circumstances, the crust is very thin and the slope becomes dangerous within minutes of the sun hitting it.

In any case, do not ski a slope if the crust is breaking.

FOG AND BAD LIGHT

In large resorts, fog may be a local phenomenon. I have skied perfect powder in the sunshine on days when it was foggy and rainy below in the village. Call the top station to find out if it is clear above, before rolling over and going back to sleep, or spending the day in a coffee bar.

If it really is foggy all over, or snowing hard, stay below the tree line. Trees break up the clouds and give definition to the scene. Without trees it can be very hard to tell up from down! Be extremely cautious in foggy conditions, I have twice had serious injuries skiing in fog, and I'm not alone. The most common

accident is hitting a road crossing a smooth slope – not fun!

Trailside markers above the tree line are there to aid skiers in fog and poor light conditions. These posts mark a trail's edge and are normally painted with fluorescent colour. The fluorescent area is generally 1m (39½in) long on right-hand posts and 30cm (12in) on the left-hand posts. This system helps skiers to keep on the trail and heading in the right direction during storms and flat light conditions.

Fog is one of the most dangerous weather conditions. Don't risk being lost; check out the trail marking system before bad weather sets in!

Trailside markers can be seen on the right side of this cat track.

8 Racing

Racing is not just for the pros. Weekly races are a popular part of many ski holidays and provide a great deal of fun for competitors of all ages. Usually organized by the ski school, weekly races offer skiers the opportunity to compete and improve technique as well as share a few laughs in a relaxed and social atmosphere.

Fig 115   Charlotte Wennberg in the lead during a fun dual telemark slalom in Verbier.

Fig 116   The start of the Derby de la Meije in La Grave, France.

DERBIES

The 'Derby' is a classic form of racing. Competitors are left to their own devices on natural, unprepared pistes without control gates. The race goes on no matter what the weather, and it's up to the racer to decide where to turn and how fast to ski.

In the Derby de la Meije, in La Grave, France, racers compete in teams, with an alpine skier, a telemarker and a snowboarder. It's a top-to-bottom race of 1,800 vertical metres! (Over 6,000 vertical feet!) In 1991 the winning time was about five minutes. That was during a blizzard!

RACING TECHNIQUE

To find out more about ski racing I spoke with Steven Lee, a downhill and super G specialist from Australia. Stevie Lee (as he is known by his many friends around the world) has been competing on the World Cup circuit since 1981.

Stevie was kind enough to take time out from a busy training schedule before the 1992 Olympics to set up gates and demonstrate racing turns for my, and I hope your, benefit. With his wealth of experience and knowledge, Stevie was able to fill me in on the latest World Cup techniques.

Stevie told me that ski-racing technique has changed considerably in the last few years with breakthroughs in ski construction and design. New technologies and materials now permit ski manufacturers to make skis with narrower sidecut for easier turning, while still maintaining sufficient torsional rigidity for exceptional grip on hard snow.

The most significant result is that racers no longer step turn. They are now able to ski a tighter, faster line by maintaining snow contact right through each turn, controlling the radius of each arc with pressure

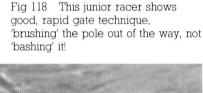

Fig 117 Stevie Lee in training. Check out the tracks from previous runs – smooth lines with no skidding at all. Angulation and anticipation are extremely important when carving a turn at 120kph (75mph).

Fig 118 This junior racer shows good, rapid gate technique, 'brushing' the pole out of the way, not 'bashing' it!

and edge angle. Increasing pressure or edge angle results in a tighter turn.

The basis of this technique is to roll both skis onto the new edge to initiate turning. If more turning is needed to make the next gate, press harder on your edges for increased ski response.

Study the racing turn to learn this technique.

RAPID GATES

In the not too distant past, slalom gates were made from bamboo. These were followed by plastic gates and now the latest version – rapid gates. Rapid gates, which have a hinge in the base, are designed to bend when struck, allowing racers to ski a more direct line by hitting the gates. Slalom racers sport plastic body armour for protection.

'Brush, don't bash.' The correct technique is to brush the pole with your plastic arm guard, not to bash it out of the way.

Fig 119(a)

Fig 119(b)

Fig 119(c)

Figs 119(a)–(h)   The racing turn.
Stevie Lee demonstrates. Stevie
simply rolls his skis from edge to
edge, maintaining a low position
throughout and carving with *both*
skis. Note how his upper body is
across the gate; this is the correct line
to take.

THE RACING TURN

In modern racing technique, racers
take advantage of improved skis to
carve continually. The turn is initiated by rolling both skis onto the
new edge at the same time. Continual carving is achieved by maintaining snow contact at all times.

Try this: descend a gentle, rolling,
open slope and simply roll both
skis from edge to edge. This results
in large radius, carved turns. To
sharpen the radius of the turn, increase edge angle and press harder on both skis.

Fig 119(f)

Fig 119(g)

Fig 119(h)

Stevie Lee.

Fig 119(d)

Fig 119(e)

Fig 120   The clean track left in the
snow after a carved turn.

Fig 121(a)

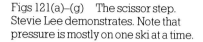

Figs 121(a)–(g)   The scissor step. Stevie Lee demonstrates. Note that pressure is mostly on one ski at a time.

Fig 121(b)

The Scissor Step Turn

Although step turns are not used much any more in World Cup racing, they are still valuable to learn as an exercise. Step turns are used to take a higher line in a race course or to avoid an obstacle.

Stevie Lee demonstrates a scissor step. It is important to create a strong platform with the outside ski, from which to step. The uphill ski is stepped or 'scissored' forwards and up the slope before being rolled immediately onto its inside edge to initiate the turn. The inside ski is brought beside the new outside ski as edging begins.

Fig 121(c)

Fig 121(d)

Fig 121(e)

Fig 121(f)

Fig 121(g)

EXERCISES FOR RACING

Below are a few exercises that will improve your skiing in preparation for racing.

Skating

Skating improves coordination and balance and develops independent leg action. *See* pages 54–55 for the photo sequences.

Skating in a figure-of-eight is another excellent exercise.

The Short Radius Turn

Skiing in the fall line trains timing and coordination. Be sure to plant your poles every turn. Make as many turns as you can, look far down the hill and don't allow your upper body to deviate from the fall line. It's fun to practise short radius turns with friends – see who can make the most turns or ski the furthest without missing a beat.

See pages 68–72 for the technique.

Ski on one Ski

This exercise is a favourite of many coaches. A short training hill with a chairlift is the perfect place to practise.

Skiing on one ski develops many skills. Obviously balance and strength are tested, but the objective is to improve the ability to roll skis on edge (invaluable for smooth, powerful, carved turns).

Leave your other ski in a safe place, at the top of the lift perhaps, and practise equally on each foot.

SKI MAINTENANCE

Well-tuned skis are easier to turn, safer and more fun to use. For op-timum performance, skis must be maintained regularly. Tuning skis is simple to do at home or even at your hotel. A ski vice and a nominal number of tools makes this task easier and more accurate.

Dry your skis after skiing to prevent edges from rusting, and run a sharpening stone over edges every couple of days. More serious burrs must be removed with a file.

To protect the base, Stevie always waxes his skis before sharpening the edges. The ski base is critical for speed – especially as races are decided by hundredths of a second. Racers have bases specially 'structured' with a diamond pattern to break resistance. Skis are passed over stone grinding machines that grind bases perfectly flat, leaving a fine texture in the surface.

Always keep bindings clean and free of mud and ice.

Waxing

Waxing protects bases and improves glide. The structure is cleaned with a copper brush before waxing. Hard wax is dripped onto the base, then melted in with an iron and scraped off with a plastic scraper when the wax is cool. The ski is then polished with a cork.

Top racers use expensive, concentrated formulas of powdered wax for maximum glide, but these don't last much longer than one run. Stevie told me that, as all racers have access to similar formulas, base structure is the most critical factor.

Edge Sharpening and Bevelling

Skis start out sharp, but quickly dull with use. For control on hard snow, skis must be kept sharp. This requires frequent attention.

To facilitate turning, edges should be slightly bevelled – filed so they are not as high as the base. A ski with edges higher than the base is 'railed' and will be difficult to turn. A bevel of one degree makes a ski pivot more easily and easier to turn. Side edges must be bevelled to stay 90 degrees to base edges.

World Cup slalom racers are the exception; their bases are ground perfectly flat and only side edges are bevelled – as much as three degrees. A ski tuned like this grips exceptionally well on ice, but is almost impossible for most skiers to turn.

A hand-held sharpening tool allows you to sharpen side edges with the same amount of bevel each time. Bottom edges are easiest to sharpen with a fine-toothed file – wrap one thickness of tape around the file to protect the base and create bevel. Sharpen each edge separately. Use long, smooth strokes to sharpen edges, and clean the file often.

Tip Colour the edge with a marker before filing to see results more easily. (Avoid touching clear bases, as these may stain.)

Stonegrinding

Before beginning to fine tune skis by hand, have them put on a stone grinder in a ski shop. A stone grinder is a machine containing a large, revolving circular stone, used to true the base. Stone grinders can also 'structure' bases for improved glide. Have your skis stoneground at the start of each season; this gives you a good surface to work on.

Naturally you can have a ski shop fine tune your skis, but this should be done often and will be expensive. Maintaining your own gear is satisfying, worth while and not difficult if you are handy with tools.

9 Telemarking

Telemark ski technique began in Norway in the late 1800s. Sondre Norheim, from the province of Telemark, is recognized as the father of the telemark turn.

Norheim made public his new technique at a jumping competition in Oslo in 1868. Completing his 23.4m (76ft) jump and stopping in a gracefully carved arc, one ski dropped back: the new telemark turn.

The technique was found to work well with the equipment of the day, free-heel bindings and wood skis with no sidecut, some of which Norheim designed. Telemarking became the predominant technique throughout and beyond Scandinavia.

By 1912, however, skiers in the Alps were beginning to descend in a different style. The Arlberg technique (developed by Hannes Schneider of the Arlberg region in Austria) had become the standard method of instruction.

By the 1940s, alpine technique had pushed ahead with a series of rapid developments and technical innovations initiated by Alpine troops defending mountain borders, and ski racers requiring a controlled, aggressive technique. The development of the 'fixed-heel' binding meant that telemarking was all but forgotten outside the rolling hills of Scandinavia.

Telemarking was 'rediscovered' in the late sixties or early seventies, by North American backcountry skiers seeking the lightest possible equipment for expeditions. Adopting the original telemark turn meant freedom from heavy alpine touring gear. 'Skinny skis' were soon introduced to lift-served terrain, not only to train for backcountry expeditions but also for the simple pleasure of the technique.

Fig 122   Telemarking. The skier is Hans Solmssen.

Fig 123   Jumping on teles! The skier is Rob Fullerton.

110

TELEMARK EQUIPMENT

At first, the new telemark skis had hardened wood edges and were fragile. Boots were low, and little sturdier than ordinary cross-country shoes. Few skiers dared to explore high, remote areas with such lightweight equipment.

Those who did, persevered, and convinced manufacturers of the future of telemarking. Ski companies listened and beefed up their telemark skis, adding steel edges. (The first telemark ski with metal edges – the XCD – was made by Karhu in 1975.) They also changed the camber from the double camber of cross-country skis to a single camber, like alpine skis. Boot makers responded to the 'new breed' telemarkers' (especially racers') need for greater performance, and boots became higher and stiffer.

The result of all this tinkering and development has been a quiet revolution. Modern-day telemark skis, boots and bindings are sophisticated pieces of equipment, wonderful to ski on.

Technical advancement in equipment has led to a large increase in the number of participants in the sport, and vice versa. Nowadays, most quality ski shops stock a small selection of telemark gear and top-of-the-line tele skis and bindings are thankfully cheaper than alpine gear.

Free-heel gear can be regarded in two categories: equipment designed for lift-served skiing/racing and that designed for off-piste skiing or touring. In practice there is considerable overlap, with many skiers touring on the same gear that they use daily. Tele gear is nothing if not versatile.

Fig 124   Telemark skis.

SKIS

Telemark skis are lighter and narrower than their alpine counterparts. The widest models are designed for touring with a heavy pack and skiing deep snow. Narrower skis are designed for skiing on piste and will perform better on firm snow and in racing.

BOOTS

Boots are the heart of modern free-heel skiing. Buy the best boots that you can afford. Unfortunately, price does dictate quality, and good telemark boots are in the same price range as top alpine boots.

Racing models, with high backs and forward lean built in, are best suited for lift-served terrain. These generally use buckles and straps for closure.

Slightly lower, more upright boots, usually closing with a combination of laces and buckles, are preferable for skiers intending to do a lot

of walking and climbing. Upright boots are more comfortable on long treks. Note that if your climbs lead you into steep powder slopes, boots with good support make it easier to recover from a bad turn, especially when carrying a pack!

Do not buy boots with lace closure only, unless most of your skiing is to be on the flat, with only occasional downhill sections.

In cold weather, an insulated gaiter is recommended for keeping feet toasty in a single boot.

Fit

Fit is always important. Free-heel skiing is not yet a mainstream sport, and finding boots can sometimes be a problem, never mind having a choice of models. This means that it can be difficult to find an alternative if your first choice is not comfortable. Luckily, tele boots are generally easy to fit for most people, and in time they adapt to the shape of your foot. Most skiers find telemark boots more comfortable than alpine boots.

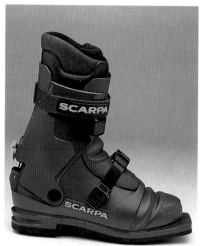

Fig 125   Telemark boots. Asolo's racing model on the left, a touring version on the right.

Fig 126   New for 1992, a plastic telemark boot from Scarpa.

For mostly lift-served skiing, a size that fits snugly with one pair of wool or capilene socks is suitable. For touring you will be warmer in boots with room enough for two pairs – a silk or synthetic (e.g. capilene) liner and a thick wool oversock. If your tours will be multi-day affairs in remote regions, consider double boots, as these are warmer and drier than single ones.

Footbeds

Telemarking requires you to be well balanced on the bottom of your foot. Custom footbeds support the whole of your foot and improve edge control. Those from your alpine boots should serve this purpose.

BINDINGS

Telemark bindings are remarkably light and simple. The free heel negates the need for a releasable binding in most falls. The exception

is racing, in which catching a tip on a gate is a distinct possibility. For this reason, many racers use bindings with a releasable plate.

There are two basic type of telemark bindings: three-pin and cable.

Three-pin Bindings

The simple three-pin system is strong and light. It is the most common form of free-heel binding. A tab in front of the boot toe and

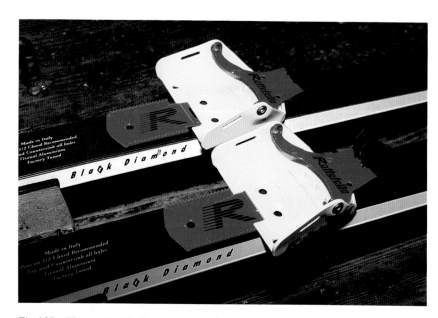

Fig 127   Three-pin bindings.

Fig 128   The telemark turn – your goal.

alpine equipment, this chapter forgoes the very basics of skiing – straight running and snowplough turns – and begins with telemark technique. For beginning skiers, the exercises in Chapter 2 will work equally well on your tele gear. Even advanced skiers will have fun trying manoeuvres from Chapter 2 on their telemark equipment.

Experienced alpine skiers should spend their first few hours on telemark equipment without worrying too much about the proper technique. Just go skiing on gentle terrain and learn to balance on lighter equipment. Skiing with less support than usual will feel strange at first (don't go down anything steep just yet!). Your alpine technique may also improve, though probably not at first.

holes in the bottom of the boot are matched with a bale and three pins on the binding. One of the best things about three-pin bindings is that they will fit any size of teleboot; they are all designed to the same 'Nordic Norm' specifications. This makes switching skis a cinch – great for ski testing.

Cable Bindings

The cable system wraps around the boot heel, pressing the toe into a clip on the front of the binding. Cable bindings, and their descendants, have been popular with ski tourers for over a hundred years. They close by tensioning the steel cable passing round the heel of the boot.

Modern cable bindings (lighter and stronger than predecessors) are often popular with more aggressive telemark skiers. The ski is kept closer to the sole when jump turning, and the binding provides additional support for high, stiff boots, protecting the soles from overflexing.

It is essential to carry a spare cable when ski touring.

POLES

Regular alpine poles are used for telemarking, but length is a personal choice. For touring, adjustable poles that connect to form an avalanche probe are the obvious solution – keep them short for downhill sections, lengthen them for climbing. On piste, I use alpine length or shorter, but short poles can be a hassle if you need to skate and pole across a long flat. Longer poles are useful for walking in deep snow.

The pole plant is not as critical in telemark technique as in alpine. You may find the old Norse solution (popular in Scandinavia), of a single, stout wooden stick, is your choice.

TECHNIQUE

Because the majority of prospective telemark skiers already ski on

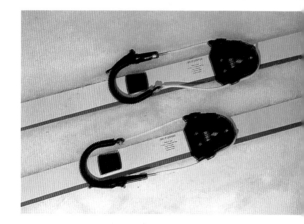

Fig 129   Riva cable bindings.

SWITCHING GEAR

I regularly switch from tele to alpine equipment (and snowboard). The first turns on either usually feel strange, as telemarking is a much looser technique than alpine skiing. Telemark skis grip hard snow less well than alpine skis, and provide less support. It's a balancing act – you literally have to switch 'gears'.

Each type of skiing teaches me something about the other. Telemarking teaches me to be graceful and to ski in balance; alpine skiing helps me to feel confident at speed and teaches me to use power. They balance each other.

THE STANCE

Stance is important. A relaxed, athletic position is best: feet shoulder width apart, with ankles, knees and hips flexed. Keep hands apart for balance.

Before putting on skis, practise walking and become familiar with the basic telemark position. This dry-land training (without skis) will give you the telemark feeling. Try the following simple exercise.

WALKING (SWING HANDS)

Stride purposefully. With each step, swing the opposite hand. As you walk, turn shoulders in the direction of the swing. Sink low as you place each step, flexing at the ankle, knee and hip, and stride into the next.

THE BASIC POSITION: JUMPING IN PLACE

Jumping in place, swinging arms and landing in a telemark stance is

Fig 130 Swing hands. Stride purposefully, swinging the opposite hand with each step.

Figs 131(a)–(d)   Jumping in place. Practise jumping in place and landing in the basic tele position.

a good way to get the feeling of the basic telemark position.

Practise jumping in place, stepping from foot to foot. Flex and extend your legs for take-off. Keep your hands well apart, for balance. This striding motion, coupled with steering the lead ski, is the basis of turning.

Weight each foot equally on landing, standing on the arch of the lead foot and ball of rear foot. This 'anticipated' stance is the basic telemark position. Most of your time on skis is spent turning, so this will be your position for much of the time. When skiing, the outside hip and leg turn the ski, while the upper body is twisted towards the fall line, anticipating the next turn.

DIAGONAL GLIDING

The next exercise is to attach your skis and go for a walk on flat terrain, with smooth packed snow. Really stride, swinging arms and shoulders and twisting your hips in the direction of each step. The left arm goes forwards with the right foot and vice versa.

Tip   Keep skis gliding on the snow at all times; don't lift them off the ground. Later this will make the transition from turn to turn much smoother and make it easier to weight both skis when edging them.

Fig 132   Diagonal striding – front view.

Figs 133(a)–(d) Diagonal striding (turn shoulders). Go for a walk on skis. Make each step a long stride, swinging your arms. Twist your hip slightly in the direction of the step.

Fig 133(b)

Fig 134 Slight turns. The left foot is forward when you are steering to the right.

SLIGHT TURNS

When comfortable with diagonal gliding, try adding a slight turning action to the lead ski.

The lead ski changes with every telemark turn. This creates a feeling of striding down the mountain. Initially (on a very shallow slope) practise switching the leading ski and then steering that ski slightly. Direct the lead ski with the inside of your front foot.

Stride down the fall line. As you step onto the forward foot, twist that foot slightly in the direction of your big toe. Put your left foot forwards when you are turning to your right, and your right foot forwards when turning to the left.

Fig 133(c)

Fig 133(d)

THE SINGLE TURN UP THE HILL

The next step in your telemark progression is to practise half turns across the fall line, gliding up the hill to stop. Gradually increase the turning radius until you are able to begin in the fall line. This 'fan progression' allows you to build up to turns in the fall line gradually.

Begin in the tele position and glide across a gentle slope. As when making slight turns, steer the lead ski by twisting your foot slightly in the direction of the turn. (Practise in both directions.)

Fig 135(a)

Figs 135(a)–(d) A single turn up the hill.

Fig 135(b)

Fig 135(d)

Fig 135(c)

Figs 136(a)–(e)   The Garland-linked
partial turns across the slope.

Fig 136(a)

Fig 136(b)

Fig 136(c)

THE GARLAND

A garland is a series of linked half turns across the hill. Linking turns comes naturally following the garland exercise. Because you are skiing across the slope, it is easy to control speed.

A garland is a combination of the previous two exercises. Make a partial turn into the fall line with the uphill ski, then stride onto your downhill ski and glide up the hill to stop. After practising one garland at a time, connect a few garlands across a gentle slope.

The garland exercise also trains you to plant your poles at the correct moment. The pole plant triggers the lead change (sliding the new forward ski into the turn). In the photo sequence this is clear during photos (a) and (b).

Fig 136(d)   Fig 136(e)

Fig 137(a)

Figs 137(a)–(e) Linked turns. On a slightly steeper slope (still very shallow), make long, round turns. Look well down the hill and think of 'big toe, little toe'.

Fig 137(b)

LINKED TURNS

After the garland exercise you will be ready to begin linking complete telemark turns. The movements are the same, but ride the ski longer for complete turns.

Above the waist, alpine and tele skiers appear similar: quiet upper body and relaxed arms. The difference in foot placement, however, completely changes the position of the hip. Tele skiers need to try even harder than alpine skiers to keep their chest and navel facing down the slope.

Turning from the hip is the key to powering a tele ski and boot. This is the biggest difference between alpine and telemark technique. In alpine, the hips face down the mountain, in the same direction as the upper body. In telemarking, the hip is twisted in the direction of the turn, and the upper body is counter-twisted downhill – this requires strong abdominal muscles!

Think 'big toe, little toe'. (This excellent advice comes from Paul Parker. For further study read his book *Freeheel Skiing*.) These simple instructions can help to solve problems with turn initiation and tracking. Focusing on the big-toe side (inside) of the front ski, and the little-toe side (outside of foot, beside the ball) of the back ski, puts pressure where it belongs and edges both skis correctly.

Slide skis from turn to turn, steering with the big-toe side of the lead ski and little-toe side of the rear ski. Stride into each turn with confidence.

Continuous movement helps to keep you in balance; at first this may feel like a series of linked recoveries – hang in there!

Fig 137(c)

Fig 137(d)

Fig 137(e)

TIPS

Simple things make a big difference on teles. Following are a few easy tips that I have found useful.

Concentrating on what you are about to do speeds learning. Focus on the task at hand.

Problem Leaning into the hill (a common mistake) results in too much weight on the inside ski.
Exercise 1 Long ago a friend of mine, Craig Hesse (a fine tele skier), told me to keep an imaginary pencil tucked in between the hip bone and waist. This keeps the upper body in balance over both skis.
Exercise 2 Carry your poles across your body in both hands (as if carrying a tray full of drinks). Descend a gentle hill, linking turns (try not to spill a drop!). This exercise will soon point out balance errors. If you tend to fall uphill, weight the ball of the back foot more.

Problem Weighting the rear ski.
Correction Keeping the rear knee tucked in close makes it possible to pressure *both* feet.

Form a pyramid with the knees as apex and pinch your buns together; this brings the knees closer together. This is a stable position allowing you to ride both skis as one long ski.

Problem The back ski slides out – it seems hard to control.
Solution Weight distribution, fore and aft, is important. Weight the entire forefoot on your back ski – press on the little-toe side. Don't keep your boot on tiptoe – with only the heel lifted – your boot should be flexed at the ball of the back foot.

Problem Turn initiation.
Solution Press more on the big-

Fig 138   Keep the rear knee tucked in close.

toe side (inside) of your front foot and steer the front ski into the turn. An early lead change (advancing the outside ski at start of turn), smooths out tele turns and places the upper body in the correct position to initiate the turn (anticipation). Think about moving the new inside ski 'out of the way' at the start of each turn.

DEEP SNOW

Skiing deep snow on telemark gear takes getting used to. If you are lucky enough to find some powder, first try descending a gentle slope, bouncing gently with weight evenly distributed on both feet. Your skis will track in a straight line.

When you feel balanced over both skis, try linking a few turns. In deep snow, skis are edged simultaneously. As you rise, keep skis flat during the lead change and edge both skis at exactly the same moment. Feel your weight between

your skis, on the heel of the front foot and ball of the rear.

Rising and sinking are very important in deep snow. Keep moving up and down; don't be stuck too low or tall. Stride from one turn to the next. The up part of the motion isn't vertical, but down the hill, diving into the fall line. Don't hold back; this motion is essential for skis to work – your upper body must feel as if it is over the downhill ski, definitely *not* leaning into the hill! Pretend that you are running downhill; keep up with your skis.

Good telemarkers use abdominal and stomach muscles to hold it all together. This is a powerful technique – especially in powder and crud. Each turn contains a wind-up, when energy is built up and a release of this energy powers you into the next turn.

Deep snow can actually help you to turn (hard to believe at first, I know). The snow builds up a platform beneath your feet, creating resistance and pushing your skis back towards you, encouraging your knees and ankles to flex – if you relax and let them. This is why your best turns will feel so smooth and 'effortless'.

Practise on an open slope – not too steep and free of rocks and trees. Twenty centimetres (8in) of fresh snow is ideal for learning. Attempt steeper and deeper slopes as you improve!

Note To control speed, make each turn a complete round arc.

A Powder Exercise

A good exercise is to practise going from a packed slope into powder and back onto the packed. As you go into the powder, weight your back foot a bit more and lean back just a little to avoid getting pitched. Returning to the packed snow, lean forwards to prepare yourself for the acceleration, and place more weight over the outside ski.

Fig 139 Anticipation on steep terrain. Note how Hans' extension is forward and down the fall line.

CRUD – THE TELE JUMP TURN

Powder and perfect piste are the exception rather than the rule and chances are there will be days when you encounter neither. For heavy snow and crud conditions the tele jump turn is the technique to use.

From a low flexed position, extend off the lower ski. Suck both skis clear of the snow with your abdominal muscles, turning them and switching the lead in mid-air. Land in the telemark position with your weight on the heel of the lead foot and ball of the rear foot to break through the crust. Make a positive pole plant to keep your upper body facing downhill.

Fig 140(e)   Make a positive pole plant to keep upper body facing downhill.

Fig 140(d)   Land in telemark position, weighting the heel front foot and ball of rear foo

Figs 140(a)–(e)   Tele jump
turns in crud.

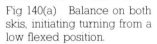

Fig 140(a)   Balance on both
skis, initiating turning from a
low flexed position.

Fig 140(b)   Plant pole and
extend off lower ski.

Fig 140(c)   Project upper
body down the fall line,
pivoting skis in the air.

TIPS FOR OFF-PISTE SKIING

1.   Wider, softer skis float more easily and are better suited to deep snow than stiff narrow skis.

2.   Weight skis evenly. Because your skis are floating in the snow, each must receive equal pressure.

3.   Project upper body down the fall line each turn. It feels like 'diving' into the fall line. Fall line skiing places you in an anticipated position, making it easier to keep your rhythm.

4.   Maintain your speed. Speed is needed for skis to begin to float. Don't hold back, control speed with the radius of your turns.

5.   Ski rhythmically, flexing and extending fully, floating from one turn to the next. Motion keeps you stable.

Figs 141(a)–(d) Anticipation is the key to steep descents.

Fig 141(a)

Fig 141(b)

STEEPS

Steep terrain is a challenge on tele-mark gear. Anticipation is the key to successful steep descents. The steeper the terrain, the further back and to the side the pole plant must be.

Chest and navel must keep facing down the hill to maintain edge grip and to prepare for the next turn. Facing in the direction of travel stores energy, which is released as you unwind.

On steeps it is even more impor-tant than usual that rising into the turn is a forward action; it feels almost like diving into the fall line. Don't hold back.

Fig 141(c)

Fig 141(d)

Figs 142(a)–(e) The tele
jump turn in spring conditions.

Fig 142(b)

ig 142(a)

The Jump Turn on
Steep Spring Snow

On steep spring-snow slopes, the
tele jump turn is used to control
speed. Skis are turned across the
fall line in the air, and do not have
time to accelerate. The photo
sequence also clearly shows
weighting both skis on landing and
a positive edge set and pole plant
in preparation for the next turn –
anticipation.

Fig 142(c)

Fig 142(d)

Fig 142(e)

BANKING – THE SURF TURN

Hans Solmssen, my model for these photo sequences, comes from the big island of Hawaii and has surfed all his life. Who better to demonstrate 'surf' technique on teles? Surf turns are great fun in smooth gullies; you can ride up and down the walls as if they were frozen waves.

To initiate a surf turn, make an early lead change (photo (b)) and bank into the turn off the uphill ski. Let go of your inside pole grip and drag a hand in the snow to increase the effect (photo (d)).

Fig 143(a)

Fig 143(c)

Fig 143(b)

Figs 143(a)–(d)   An Hawaiian-style surf turn.

Fig 143(d)

PARALLEL TURNS

There is no rule book to say that you can only do telemark turns when using tele gear (except when racing). I often use parallel turns in powder, also on steep and narrow terrain. As tele equipment is less stable and powerful than alpine gear, more finesse is required for parallel turns.

Tips 1. A flexed ankle is more stable laterally, allowing the knee to act as a shock absorber. Ankle flexion and extension is also the answer to unweighting skis in a parallel turn.

2. In deep snow you must be very centred over both feet at all times.

Note For more advice on parallel turns, study the sections on alpine technique.

TOURING

Tele gear is light, and it is easy to slip on climbing skins or put skis on your shoulder and search out un-tracked powder slopes. Touring is one of the best reasons to get onto telemark equipment. You can escape the crowds and observe nature close up.

For more advice on off-piste skiing, see Chapter 6.

Fig 145 'Skinning' up the mountain.

Fig 146 The descent.

Fig 144 Attaching synthetic 'seal' skins for climbing.

TELEMARK RACING

Attending a telemark race provides a great opportunity to improve technique and meet other telemarkers. The people who telemark are a fun crowd, and races usually include lots of partying and good times.

Like alpine racing, tele races are determined by time, but penalty points are accrued for each parallel turn (usually one second is added per parallel turn). For extra excitement, telemark races sometimes include an uphill section and a jump.

There is also national-level telemark racing in some countries, and a world championship.

Fig 147 Telemark racing.

10 Snowboarding

Snowboarding is skiing, skateboarding and surfing, all wrapped up in one. It began in the sixties with the Snurfer. Snurfers were the invention of American surfer named Sherman Poppen. He sold the idea to Brunswick Sporting Goods, which marketed Snurfers for $15 apiece. They were shorter and wider than a snow ski, more like a single water-ski, without bindings. The Snurfer was a very simple piece of fun. A handle attached to a rope in front and a traction pad were the sole improvisations for balance.

A 'Snurf freak' named Jake Burton attached rubber straps to his board for better control. The result was a breakthrough that led Jake to start a company in Vermont, making laminated wooden boards. Meanwhile, on the west coast, skateboard world champion Tom Sims also began snowboard production, and back in New York, Dimitrije Milovich, an engineer, formed Winterstick to make epoxy/fibreglass boards. It was the mid-seventies and snowboarding was on its way as a popular sport.

Though the new 'snowboards' generated much excitement among a growing group of *cognoscenti*, most lift companies failed to respond enthusiastically. Snowboarders were not allowed to ride many lifts or even be in ski-area boundaries. Perhaps the lift companies were fearful of lawsuits, or maybe just unresponsive to this new crowd for traditional reasons. Snowboarders were often younger than the resorts' regular clientele and often skateboarders and surfers, not skiers. These restrictions stalled growth of the sport. If you wanted to ride, you had to walk. If you've ever tried wading through deep snow, or climbing in snowshoes, you'll realize that the original snowboarders were hard core. It wasn't until the mid-eighties that most lift companies had a change of heart (or accountant).

Technical innovations in the mid-eighties made boards easier to ride and widened their commercial

Fig 148   Matt Gilder riding a frozen wave.

Fig 149   In the early days of the sport, riding meant walking – most resorts did not permit snowboarders on the lifts.

market. Steel edges, plastic bases, high top bindings (similar to today's soft bindings), and ski touring bindings (the predecessor of plate bindings) combined with touring boots, were all major improvements that greatly improved control.

In the eighties, Burton and Sims began to expand into Europe, and many new companies were formed. Demand grew fast; it was the right sport at the right time. Chamonix, France (already home to a number of monoskiers), became Europe's snowboarding mecca, and the dream of surfing the Alps was realized.

In 1986, a group of keen riders began organizing races world-wide. This led to the first world championships in 1987. The World Cup circuit began in 1988, elevating awareness of the sport internationally. By 1989 there were 1.5 million people snowboarding – double the number of

Fig 150   Air.

the previous season – forty per cent of them in North America. (Industry Statistics Sheet, National Snowboard Inc., Englewood, Colorado, 1990.) Today, snowboard schools and camps can be found in most resorts,

and a number of magazines keep up with the sport's new developments.

While the original snowboarders were well outside the mainstream, riders now represent a complete

131

Fig 151 A qualified instructor can make learning to snowboard safer and easier.

(For further information contact Dr Riyad B. Abu-Laban, Mineral Springs Hospital, PO Box 1050, Banff, AB TOL OCO, Canada.)

The fact that most of the injured snowboarders were also alpine skiers suggests that many novice snowboarders may tend to exceed the limits of their skill by snowboarding on terrain that they feel comfortable on with skis. In addition, as with skiing, most of the injuries occurred in the afternoon, when fatigue was likely to be a factor.

ALPINE OR FREESTYLE?

There are two streams in the snowboarding world – alpine and freestyle.

Freestyle riding incorporates trick moves and half-pipe riding. A half pipe is a snowy gully, usually artificially made. It is a similar, but larger, version of those used by skateboarders. There are many similarities between freestyle and skateboard moves.

Alpine riders descend mountains like skiers (though using terrain differently). This chapter is dedicated to alpine riding techniques. Soft (freestyle) equipment can also be used for alpine riding.

EQUIPMENT

Snowboarding equipment is simple: a board, boots, warm dry clothing and sunglasses, and you are all set.

BOARDS

Snowboard construction is similar to that of skis. Indeed, most snowboards are made by ski manufacturers. The difference between

Fig 152 Snowboarding equipment is simple: a board, boots, warm dry clothing and sunglasses, and you are all set. Matt Gilder and Kiki Thompson.

alpine and freestyle boards is not construction, but design. Freestyle boards have less usable edge due to turned-up tails and noses (tail kick and nose kick). Race boards have the longest effective edge length, with little nose kick and no tail kick.

Half-pipe Boards

The shortest boards are half-pipe boards, ranging from 140cm (55in) to 165cm (65in). With an effective edge length of under 110cm, (43in) and a distinctive narrow-waisted outline, these boards are best for trick riding, slow speeds and jumping. They have the most tail and nose kick, and are normally ridden with soft boots and shell bindings to match their easy turning characteristics. Half-pipe boards can also perform well in moguls.

cross-section, from sporty grandparents to kids. Juniors especially are the sport's keenest fans.

One of the great things about snowboarding is its relatively simple technique. It is not a complicated discipline to master. The first two or three days can be typically frustrating (and punishing), but the rise to competence is usually rapid, and accessible to all who try. Survive the first three days and you won't look back!

Remember, a qualified instructor can make learning safer and less of an ordeal. A survey of snowboard accident victims was taken at Mineral Springs Hospital in Banff, Alberta, Canada over two seasons (1988–90) (in *Canadian Medical Association Journal*, vol. 145, no. 9). Results showed that thirty-six per cent of those surveyed had never been on a snowboard previously, and another twenty-five per cent were in their first year of the sport.

Allround Boards

Available in many sizes, this is the largest board category. Allround boards can be divided into 'free-style' and 'alpine' oriented boards.

Freestyle Oriented Boards These are slightly longer, (from 150cm to 165cm((59in to 65in) than half-pipe boards, with a greater effective edge length, up to 125cm (49in). They have a long shovel radius and moderate tail kick. A good choice as a first board, freestyle oriented boards can be used for occasional half-pipe practice, as well as for trick riding and jumping.

Alpine Oriented Boards From 150cm to 170cm (59in to 67in) long, these are suitable for riders of all abilities from beginners up. Effective edge length is from 110cm to 135cm (43in to 53in). With medium shovel radius and small tail kick, these boards are designed to perform well in all snow conditions, including powder.

Raceboards

Either symmetric or asymmetric in shape, with the longest gliding surface, raceboards often show up on the market direct from testing on the World Cup circuit. From 155cm to 180cm (61in to 71in) long, and with an effective edge length of 130cm to 160cm (51in to 63in), raceboards are designed for speed and carving. With short shovels and no tail kick, they grip well on hard snow. Raceboards require good technique; their ability to carve is appreciated by experienced riders. The carving ability of a good raceboard is nothing short of phenomenal.

There is a strong trend for asymmetric raceboards. Longer on the rider's backside than front, they

certainly look interesting. On the World Cup circuit, riders are winning with both symmetric and asymmetric boards, so I would say that the jury is still out. Other factors, such as flex and torsional rigidity, seem to have more direct influence on performance.

Note As with skis, overall flex, torsional resistance and sidecut are the most important design details affecting a board's performance. There is no standard formula to guarantee that a board will suit you perfectly. When comparing similar boards, brief ski-shop staff, magazine reviews, promotional material and other riders for information. Most good ski shops have demonstration models available. *Try before you buy.*

BOOTS

Boots and bindings work together as a system. They are either 'hard' or 'soft'. Hard systems use simple clip bindings and boots similar to alpine ski touring boots. Soft systems use snow boots and rely on the shell of the binding for support.

Hard Boots

Hard boots are similar to ski mountaineering boots and require very simple bindings. Many alpine riders prefer hard boots, which provide good control on firm snow. Hard boots are necessary if crampons will be used to access remote peaks.

The best are asymmetric in design – the liner of the front boot being substantially higher and stiffer than the rear liner. The uppers of these boots can also be changed to adjust flex. To avoid shops having to stock asymmetric boots in twice as many pairs, the foot sections of the liners are symmetric and fit both

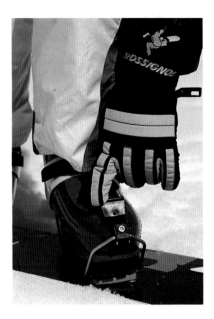

Fig 153   A 'hard' boot with Emery binding.

the left and right foot. By switching the liner from boot to boot, they can be used by either regular (left foot forward) or 'goofy' (right foot forward) riders.

Soft Boots

Soft boots allow for greater movement than hard ones and are the system of choice for freestyle tricks and half-pipe riding. They are also comfortable in deep powder snow, where edging precision is not critical.

Soft systems rely on the binding shell, which wraps around the boots for support. The most popular type of boots used are bootpacs, such as Sorels – a Canadian design, with rubber bottoms and leather tops, lined in felt. Bootpacs are very warm and comfortable. Soft boots are popular among those who exclusively ride off piste in deep snow, and are the best choice if your expect to be climbing using snowshoes.

Fig 154   A Rossignol snowboard boot.

Fig 155   A Wombat 'soft' boot shell binding.

BINDINGS

Most snowboard bindings are designed not to release. Snowboards have a substantial swing weight, and injury is likely if one binding releases, leaving the other foot attached to a spinning board. A strap, attaching board to leg, is essential in the unlikely event that a binding should come off. A runaway board is a serious hazard. This strap also proves useful when carrying the board.

Binding Placement

Snowboard bindings are placed fore and aft on the board with the rider standing sideways. In the past, riders stood with their feet at a greater angle to the board than is currently popular. With the production of better carving boards, many people are adopting a stance that is more in line with the central axis of their board.

The type of riding that you prefer will determine the binding angles that you use. Precision of binding placement is very important, even for beginners. Correct placement ensures a position that is comfort-able and avoids strain. A few centimetres can make the difference between an awkward or a more natural position.

It may take some experience before you find your ideal foot placement. As some normal bindings are not very adjustable, consider using rental boards to sample various positions.

REGULAR OR GOOFY?

Aspiring snowboarders must first determine whether they are regular or goofy. This has nothing to do with Mickey Mouse. The original snowboarders were surfers, and much of the terminology stems from California beach talk. A regular stance (also called natural) is with left foot

Fig 156   Kiki, in yellow, rides goofy with her right foot forward. Matt, in red, is regular, with his left foot forward.

forward; most people feel more in balance this way. Goofy footers stand with the right foot forward. If you surf or skateboard, you will already know which you are. Everybody else needs to work this out.

Your foot preference in other sports should indicate your natural inclination on a snowboard. If you kicked a football, would you balance on your left foot and kick with your right? Descending on a mountain bike, would you keep your left foot forward? If so, you are probably regular (natural). Goofy footers are more likely to kick with their left foot and balance better on their right. Another test is to have a friend give you a gentle push from behind – regular riders are more likely to step forwards with their left foot.

Go out a few times on a snowboard and you will know for sure. Standing opposite to your natural inclination gives the sensation of going backwards.

BINDING ADJUSTMENT

The rider's height determines the width apart of binding placement. This distance is about the same for both freestyle and alpine riding, though freestylers (using shell bindings) may prefer to place their bindings a further two to three centimetres (about an inch) apart.

Height	Stance
155cm (61in)	37cm (14½in)
160cm (63in)	38cm (15in)
165cm (65in)	39cm (15½in)
170cm (67in)	40cm (16in)
175cm (69in)	41cm (16½in)
180cm (71in)	42cm (17in)
185cm (73in)	43cm (17½in)
190cm (75in)	44cm (18in)

Rider	Angle in degrees	
	Front	Rear
Racers, experts, very small boards, large boot sizes	45–50	38–45
Allround, piste, deep snow, beginners	40–45	30–35
Freestyle, half-pipe (soft bindings)	25–40	15–20

Placement Angles

Generally, beginners prefer to stand more across their boards than racers and advanced riders do. As you will not be a beginner for long, it may be worthwhile to rent first. Rental bindings are adjustable, and drilling extra holes in your new board is not recommended. A more forward-facing position is likely to appeal to skiers. If you are an experienced skateboarder or surfer, naturally you will know your preferred stance.

Canting

Small wedges beneath your feet place you in a more natural position. Cants lift up the outside of your feet, pushing your knees closer together. This slight triangulation gives you a stronger stance. Cants are generally used under the rear foot and are usually supplied with bindings for hard boots. The front binding should be mounted flat, or perhaps with one or two thin washers under the leading edge.

Accessories

Traction pads, usually essential, are pads of corrugated rubber between the front and rear bindings. They provide grip for the rear foot when you are skating or riding a lift.

Special protective equipment to reduce risk of injury is commonly worn by racers. Beginners – who often fall awkwardly at first – and riders with problematic spines should protect themselves. Available equipment includes gloves with built-in wrists and thumb protectors, knee pads, hip pads, etc., and back protectors – the same type used by parapente (paraglider) pilots.

Clothing

Snowboarders spend more time than skiers in direct contact with the snow. Sitting down to rest (there are no poles to lean on); using hands surfer style to push through the snow or grace a turn; changing direction in place; going from sitting to kneeling; all add up to cold and wet body parts!

Gloves should be tough, long and waterproof. Loose-fitting pants should also be waterproof and well insulated. Jackets or sweaters must be warm, long and large for movement. It goes without saying that cool sunglasses are mandatory.

SAFETY

Safety is a matter of self-preservation as well as consideration for others.

Take responsibility for your own board and actions.

In particular:

1. Rest only to the side of the slope.
2. Make sure that you can be seen by those uphill – being run over is no fun!
3. Wear a runaway strap.
4. Don't leave your board where it may slide away.
5. Always be aware of others.

For further information on safety and proper slope etiquette, read The Skier's Code at the beginning of the book – the same rules apply to snowboarders as to other slope users.

SNOWBOARD TECHNIQUE

The Progression

The following snowboard progression was explained to me by Matt Gilder, a very experienced snowboarding instructor from Australia. Matt was also kind enough to teach the progression to me, and I found his method extremely effective. I hope you find the same. Matt is demonstrating in the photo sequences.

The basic skills of snowboarding are pressure control, pivoting and edging. This section helps to develop each of these skills in easy stages. Snowboards are much wider than skis and turn differently, more like surfboards. The rider balances on the front foot and steers with the rear. The movement is fluid, definite, not rushed.

Pressure Control

The skill of weighting and unweighting your board is called pressure control. At beginner's level, the movement of rising (standing taller) is used to reduce pressure, and momentarily unweight the board, so that turns can be initiated.

Lowering your body position increases pressure, digging the edge of your board into the snow. This provides lateral resistance to push against. Stand lower when finishing a turn.

Note It is the up and down movement, not the positions themselves, that changes the load on the board.

Pivoting

The board pivots about the front foot during the transition from one turn to the next. It is a key movement during a low-speed turn.

Edging

Edging is the application of pressure to a snowboard's edge. The process of edging enables the rider to exploit a board's shape and flex. When a moving snowboard is placed on edge, it will turn. Increasing pressure on the edge turns the board more sharply.

TERRAIN

Throughout this chapter you will see reference to the ideal terrain for learning each manoeuvre. It is important to practise on easy terrain until you feel very comfortable. This will encourage a freer style, with less braking, as you advance.

STATIONARY EXERCISES

The object of stationary exercises is to review skills that will be used when riding, without complicating matters by sliding down a slope.

Before starting with the exercises, do a gentle warm-up. Everyone, whether beginner or expert, should warm up at the start of every session.
Tips 1. When leaving your board in the snow, don't stand it up as you would a pair of skis: it could easily fall and slide away. Lay it in the snow, binding side down.
2. Check that bindings fit boots, before heading up the mountain; they may be impossible to adjust without tools.

THE STANCE

The basic snowboarding stance is a relaxed, athletic position. Ankles, knees and hips are flexed, with head and shoulders facing down the slope. All movements come from and return to this neutral position. Keep your arms apart, raised to-

Fig 157 The basic stance. In a neutral stance, most of your weight is on the front leg.

wards the front, for balance. In a neutral stance, most of your weight is on the front leg.

Balance on the Front Foot – Without Board

When riding a snowboard you balance on your front foot and steer with the rear.

To get the feeling of balancing on your front foot, do several one-legged knee bends (on flat terrain) using your front foot only.

Balance on Front Foot – on Board

Now attach the front binding and repeat the one-legged knee bends, flexing your knee and ankle. Keep your head up and upper body relaxed. Notice that boots and board provide a lot of support.

Fig 158   Balance on the front foot. Keep your head up and upper body relaxed. Practise one-legged knee bends while balancing on your front foot.

Figs 159(a) and (b)   Pressure control.

Fig 159(a)   Lowering your body position increases pressure. Stand lower in preparation for turning and when finishing a turn.

Fig 159(b)   By rising, pressure on the board is reduced. This makes it easier to start turning.

Pressure Control

Practise pressure control, by weighting and unweighting a stationary board. Lowering your body position to weight your board (increase pressure), as in preparation for turning and when finishing a turn. (As turns are linked, the posi-tion is the same.) Then raise body position to unweight your board (decrease pressure) – as when starting a turn.

Note   It is the *rhythmic movement* of rising and sinking, that changes pressure on your board. You must continually rise and sink, to initiate and finish turns.

Figs 160(a) and (b)   Swivel hips.

Fig 160(a)   Turn hips and torso to face right.

Fig 160(b)   Turn hips and torso to face left.

Swivel Hips

Initially when snowboarding, the hips, and the upper body are used to initiate turns. This is different from most ski techniques. Remember – slow and steady movements are the rule when learning to snowboard.

Slowly turn your hips and upper body to face left and right. This is how you will move your upper body to begin a turn.

SKATING

Snowboards are easy to push along on the flat. This exercise gives you a good feeling for balancing on your front foot while moving. Unclip the rear binding and use your back foot to push yourself along.

This is similar to propelling a scooter or skateboard. After each push, rest your foot back on the board and glide as far as you can. A traction pad between the bindings makes this easier. Keep your hands out and head up. Looking ahead improves balance – don't look at your feet.

Find an open area away from other snowboarders and skiers to practise skating back and forth on the flat, before progressing to the following exercises. It is easier to skate on firm packed snow than in untracked snow.

Fig 161(a) and (b)   Skating. Unclip the rear binding and use your back foot to push yourself along.

CLIMBING

When first learning to snowboard, stick to gentle slopes and climb for each run. You can start to ride lifts as soon as you feel in control.

Sidestepping

Facing the slope and with your rear foot out of the binding, step up a gentle slope. Keep the board across the slope and dig in its edge to avoid sliding. Take small steps.

Fig 163   Walking. Sidestepping is useful for climbing small distances. For greater altitude carry your board; it's easier.

Fig 162   Sidestepping. Keep the board across the slope and dig in its edge to avoid sliding. Take small steps.

GLIDING (STRAIGHT RUNNING)

Most of your weight must be on the front foot when riding. The *main* exercise at this stage (don't skip this one!) is to slide down a very gentle slope balanced on your front foot, keeping your rear foot off the board. Choose a slope that ends in a flat area, and glide as far as you can.

After gliding on one foot, practise with both feet on the board. Leave the rear binding undone at this stage (watch that the bales don't drag in the snow).

Finally, attach both bindings and descend again. Continue this exer-

Fig 164   Gliding on one foot.

Fig 165   Gliding on both feet.

Fig 166(a)

Fig 166(b)

Figs 166(a)–(f)   Turn over/getting up from a fall. To turn over, kick up your front foot and roll over on your side. When facing the slope, push yourself up with your hands.

cise until you feel in balance on your front foot.

Now repeat the exercise, marginally increasing your altitude and with both feet in the bindings.

Note   Choose a slope where you can glide a short distance before coasting to a stop.

FALLING

Falling is part of learning (at all levels). Expect to fall and don't be disheartened.

To avoid catching an edge as you slide, lift both feet, and go with the motion. Keep smiling!

Fig 166(c)

Turning Over or Getting up from a Fall

After a fall, you may not be facing in your original direction. To turn over, kick up your front foot to roll over on your side. When facing the slope, push yourself up with your hands. To turn back onto your seat, roll in the opposite direction. Always roll the board on its tail.

Attaching the Board on a Slope

On moderate slopes, dig a small platform in the snow to prevent the board from sliding away. On steeper slopes it is easier to attach your board while sitting down.

140

Fig 167 Frontside/backside. Kiki, riding goofy, is traversing (crossing) the slope backside. Matt, riding natural, is traversing frontside.

FRONTSIDE/BACKSIDE

When your back is towards the slope you are riding backside; when facing the slope, you are frontside. This distinction gains importance as you progress. Practise all manoeuvres frontside *and* backside!

Fig 166(d)

Fig 166(e)

Fig 166(f)

SIDESLIPPING

Sideslipping allows you to move sideways in a controlled slide down the hill. The skill of edge control is trained by this exercise.

Find a smooth, moderate slope. Begin in your neutral position, balanced on the uphill edge of your board. Keeping the edge of the board angled into the slope keeps you from sliding. Flatten the board slightly to release the edge, and slide downhill. To stop sliding, roll the board back on edge. When riding backside, stand tall and roll on to your heels, digging the edge into the slope, When riding frontside, roll on to your toes, pushing knees towards slope.

Note Practise sideslipping in both directions; they are quite different. With the hill behind you, it is easy to see where you are going. Facing the hill, you'll need to look over your shoulder.

PIVOTING

Pivoting the board is used to change direction at slow speeds. On a flat

Fig 169 Pivoting. Balance on your front foot. Push and pull the board with your rear foot, pivoting about the front.

Figs 168(a) and (b) Sideslipping.

Fig 168(a) Frontside.

Fig 168(b) Backside.

slope, away from traffic, practise pivoting the board underfoot to develop the skill of steering. This skill is essential. Undo the rear binding, balance on your front foot, then push and pull the board with the rear foot.

FAN PROGRESSION

A fan progression encourages learning at a comfortable pace. Proceed from a slight change of direction while crossing the hill to a turn in the fall line, taking a slightly steeper line each run. There is no need to go on steeper slopes until you are feeling at ease.

Directional Sideslip

Crossing the slope diagonally, moving both downhill and forwards, is called a directional sideslip. This is the first exercise in the fan pro-

gression. Practise your directional sideslip in both directions on a wide, gentle slope. Stand tall and roll the board on edge to stop.

Fig 170 Directional sideslip. Feel the edge 'brushing the snow' as your board drifts downhill and across the slope. Edge a little harder to stop.

The Falling Leaf

Think of your board as an autumn leaf falling from a tree. Adding a little pivoting action to a directional sideslip is called a falling leaf exercise. Use a very gentle slope.

It sounds cute, but the object is to make little half turns, without having to commit yourself to the speed generated in the fall line. It is similar to a christie garland in skiing jargon.
Note Rise to start pivoting and sink as you pressure the edge.

Figs 171(a)–(d) The falling leaf. Half turns while crossing the slope.

Fig 171(b)

Fig 171(c)

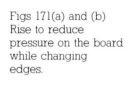

Figs 171(a) and (b) Rise to reduce pressure on the board while changing edges.

Fig 171(a)

Fig 171(d)

Figs 171(c) and (d) Sink to put pressure on the new edge.

Figs 172(a)–(c) The backside turn up the hill.

Fig 172(a) Begin in a low position and rise to reduce pressure on the board.

Fig 172(b) Steer the board with your rear foot – pivoting it about your front foot.

Fig 172(c) Finish the turn by using heel pressure to progressively edge the board. Glide up the hill to stop.

144

First Turns

The easiest way to think of a turn is to break it down into its parts. There are three stages to a turn: preparation (standing tall to lighten the board), pivoting (steering by twisting the board), and edging (rolling the board on edge).

Turning requires all the skills that you have been developing.

Preparation A low, balanced position gives you a good base from which to rise into your next turn. Rise to reduce pressure on the board, turning your head and torso towards the inside of the turn.

Steering Push or pull the back of the board with your rear foot (pivot about the front foot) to steer.

Edging Increase the edge angle by leaning towards the inside of the turn, pressing on your heels if you are riding backside or toes if riding frontside.

A turn feels like this: Ride the uphill edge. Flex, sinking low on your board. Rise, turn your head and torso and look in the direction of the turn. Roll the board onto the new edge (rock on your toes or heels). Pivot about your front foot, and steer with the rear foot. Push against the new edge, sink low to increase pressure.

The Turn up the Hill

Begin the fan progression with a slight change of direction. Matt, demonstrating this manoeuvre, has attached only his front binding, to emphasize balancing on the front foot.

To focus balancing weight on the front foot, Matt repeats the gliding on front foot exercise, lifting his rear foot completely off the board for a moment before placing it back on the board and turning up the hill to stop.

Figs 173(a) and (b) The frontside turn up the hill. A frontside turn is the same as a backside turn (in the opposite direction), but edge pressure is applied through the knees and toes instead of the heels.

Fig 174 Problems. The most common problem at this stage is to weight the wrong foot (the rear foot). Note that Kiki also has her hands back – keep the hands forward.

Fig 175(e) Control the radius of the turn with the rear foot.

Fig 175(d) Keep your hands forward and balance on the front foot.

Fig 175(c) Pivot the board about your front foot, transferring pressure from heels to toes as you do so.

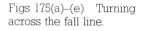

Figs 175(a)–(e) Turning across the fall line.

Fig 175(a) Start slipping diagonally across the slope, then sink low to prepare for turning.

Fig 175(b) Rise, turning your upper body and hips in the direction of the next turn.

The Complete Turn across the Fall Line

Gradually increase the radius of each turn up the hill until you can comfortably make round turns. The next stage is to make a turn completely across the fall line. Connect both bindings for this exercise.

Patience is a virtue. All movements must be slow and definite. Allow a moment for the board to come round. Don't rush your turns; use a wide, gentle slope with spacious runout.

Fig 176(a)   Allow the board to drift on its uphill edge.

Figs 176(a)–(c)   Linked turns with directional sideslip.

Linked Basic Turns

Rising and sinking, twisting and turning: this is where it all comes together. Once you feel confident turning in both directions, begin linking your turns together. Start by linking two turns with a directional sideslip, and build on that. To control speed, be sure to complete each turn – turn the board completely across the fall line every time.

A smooth, wide, gentle slope is ideal.

Fig 176(b)   Turn shoulders and hips to initiate your next turn.

Fig 176(c)   Allow the board to drift on its near uphill edge.

148

Fig 177(a)

Fig 177(b)

Fig 177(c)

Figs 177(a)–(f) Linked basic turns.
Aim to make your turns as smooth
and rhythmic as possible. Remember,
be patient, relax and allow time
for the board to come around.
All movements must be slow and
definite.

Fig 177(d)

Fig 177(e)

Fig 177(f)

RIDING LIFTS

While cable cars and telecabines are the easiest lifts for a snowboarder to ride, they are not often used to service beginner slopes. Chances are, the slopes you'll be learning on have chairlifts, pomas or T-bars.

Chairlifts are simple, and you can usually remove your board if you are worried about unloading. Surface lifts are initially more difficult; you'll need to keep your balance while being dragged up the hill. Don't ride drag lifts (T-bars and pomas) until you feel confident sliding. Begin by riding short lifts, that go up gentle slopes only – steepness makes drag lifts harder to ride.

Looking ahead will help you to stay in the track. If you should fall,

let go of the T-bar or poma and get off the track as quickly as possible. Be ready to unload as you near the top of the lift. Release the T-bar with your inside hand and slide away from the unloading area immediately.

When first riding lifts, be careful not to bite off more than you can chew – fatigue and frustration hinder progress. Stick to short runs and very easy terrain at first.

T-Bars and Pomas

For comfort, experienced riders often unclip the rear binding before riding the lift. (Check that no part of the binding will drag in the snow.) When learning, I found it easier to keep both bindings clipped – it's a personal choice. If you are riding

Fig 179 Riding with a skier or experienced snowboarder gives added support. The rider with his back to the centre bar places the T-bar behind his front leg from the other side.

Figs 178(a)–(c) Riding the T-bar.

Fig 178(a) Slide up to the loading area and turn your torso to face the approaching T-bar. Pull down on the T-bar as it arrives.

Fig 178(b) Place it between your legs so that it will pull your front leg.

Fig 178(c) There may be a strong pull when starting. Hold on firmly with both hands, but don't pull back or sit.

Fig 180 Riding a poma. The principal difference between riding a poma and T-bar is that T-bars are permanently attached to the moving cable, and pomas detach at the loading area. Looking ahead helps balance.

with only one binding attached, a traction pad is essential. Some lift companies do not permit riding with only one foot attached; always follow the lift attendant's instructions.

CARVING

The next stage in learning to snowboard is to consolidate your technique and learn to carve turns. Carving means to cut a turn using the edge of the board for resistance. The harder you press on the edge, and the greater the edge angle, the sharper the radius of your turn will be. Alpine snowboards do this very well. With speed, a rider can place the board at an extreme angle to the snow, greatly increasing the carving effect. Practise on a smooth, moderate open slope.

Figs 181(a) and (b)   Carving.

Fig 181(a)

Fig 181(b)

Anticipation

For smooth carved turns, begin to lean your upper body into the turn before changing edges. This sets you up correctly for the turn and is known as 'anticipation'.

Figs 182(a) and (b)   Anticipation.

Figs 183(a)–(d)   Short radius
turns. Rhythmic flexion and
extension is the key to short
radius turns.

Fig 183(a)   Extension.

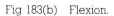

Fig 183(b)   Flexion.

Fig 183(c)   Extension.

Fig 183(d)   Flexion.

Short Radius Turns

Good rhythm is required for short
radius turns. Keep your upper body
in the fall line, belly button pointing
to the valley, and let the board swing
out from side to side. As with longer
radius turns, rise to unweight, and
sink to edge. Try to make turns of
equal radius in both directions.
Note   Practise on shallow pitches
and work on developing rhythm
before going on to steeper terrain.

Fig 185(b)

Fig 185(c)

Fig 185(d)

Fig 184   The Vitelli turn.

The Vitelli Turn

A turn with extreme body lean, the Vitelli turn is named after Serge Vitelli, the French World Cup snowboarder, who brought recognition to the manoeuvre.

The Vitelli turn requires excellent board-handling skills and a board that carves well, preferably an alpine raceboard.

Find a smooth slope of moderate pitch (not too steep). Practise short swing turns using extra down and up motion. On good, grippy snow, gradually increase your commitment of lean into the turn and turning radius.

Fig 185(a)

Figs 185(a)–(h)   Vitelli turn sequence.

Fig 185(e)

Fig 185(f)

Fig 185(h)

Fig 185(g)

Fig 186 Speed. Bend into a low, tucked, forward-leaning position, with hands behind your back or held close to your body. Keep your head up.

Bend into a low, tucked, forward-leaning position, with your hands behind your back or held close to your body. Keep your head up. For maximum glide, edge as little as possible, keeping the board flat on the snow.

Going fast is easy, slowing down calls for a little more skill. Rise slowly from your tuck, leaning forwards to accept the deceleration. Make long, sweeping turns to stop. A slope ending in a gentle rise is easier to slow down on.

If you fall on your side, slide, being sure to keep the board well clear of the snow. If you catch an edge and begin to tumble, go with it (you won't have much choice: it'll be sky snow sky snow sky, etc. until you are able to stop). Relax!

Note I advocate everybody pushing their personal limits but it's not necessary to be the fastest on the slope. If 30kph (18mph) is 'pushing the envelope' (extending yourself and exploring your personal limits),

SPEED

The ability to go fast is a real asset on a snowboard and can save much walking across flats; besides, speed is fun. For safety's sake, keep speed down if the trail is narrow or rocky. Don't practise going fast on crowded slopes or pass close to those who are moving more slowly. Choose a wide, open slope, preferably one ending in a rise (this makes slowing down easier). Check that it is clear of traffic, and let it rip.

Fig 187 Falling.

Fig 188 Snowboarding in powder.

that's great, go for it! Increase speeds gradually to develop skills and confidence.

Tip Whenever you have the opportunity, try following a faster rider. Many people experience unexpected breakthroughs following someone a little faster (or much faster) than themselves.

At least three things happen when you follow an expert rider.

1.   Your line is chosen for you – he made that turn, so can you.
2.   This is the best opportunity to learn in an instinctive manner. Try to follow turn for turn; when you are following, don't think too hard about what's going on, rather try to move the same way as the person who you are following.
3.   Having gone a little bit faster, the next time that you ride on this slope, your speed threshold will be greater.

POWDER SNOW

Snowboards do not require a special technique for powder, though you must balance further back to avoid digging in the tip, especially if the snow is very deep. Ride on steeper slopes to maintain speed – deep snow provides more resistance. Be sure to wax the base of your board to ensure easy sliding.

The most important thing to know about powder is that it is potentially deadly – avalanches are nothing to play with. It is easier to learn to descend powdery slopes on a snowboard than on skis. Neophyte riders with little experience in high mountains can quickly find themselves in a dangerous situation. Read chapter 7 for more information and try to learn as much as you can.

Have fun shredding!

Glossary

Angulation, angulated The lateral angle created between parts of the body.

Anticipation Turning the upper body to face towards the inside of the turn before turning skis.

Avalement Flexing and extending legs to maintain contact with the snow and absorb bumpy terrain.

Braquage Pivoting skis across the line of travel while flexing rapidly.

Carving Turning with little sideways slipping of skis, using ski's edges to maximum effect.

Cat track A gentle trail winding down the mountainside, providing access for novice skiers and snowcats.

Christie Any skidded turn or part of a skidded turn with skis parallel.

Counter rotation Twisting the upper body in the opposite direction to the lower.

Down unweighting Reducing pressure on skis by flexing legs. Note: The quicker legs are flexed, the stronger the effect.

Edge control Using the angle created between skis and the slope to control steering and braking.

Edging Placing skis on edge for steering or braking.

Edge set The moment during a quick turn or stop when edges are pressed hard against the snow. Setting the edge makes snow fly from beneath skis.

Extension Extending or straightening legs to control pressure of skis on the snow.

Fall line The imaginary line down a slope that a rolling ball would follow. This term normally describes the general inclination of a slope not a specific point on the snow.

Fan progression Using a series of progressive manoeuvres to develop skills: beginning with a shallow traverse, moving on to a turn in the fall line and eventually leading to complete turns.

FIS. Fédération Internationale de Ski. International body responsible for regulating skiing and ski competition.

Flexion Flexing ankles and knees to control pressure on skis. Rapid flexion unweights skis. Flexion is also used to absorb bumps and to create a 'platform' for up-unweighting.

Garland A series of linked partial turns executed while skiing across a slope.

Inertia The property of matter that makes it remain in place or continue in motion unless influenced by external forces.

Inclination Inclining the body to the inside of the turn to counteract inertia felt during a turn.

Initiation The moment when the skier begins to turn skis.

Inside ski The ski which is nearest to the inside of a turn.

Neutral position Balanced, ready for action. Facing forward, ankles knees and hips flexed, hands up and apart.

Outside ski The ski which is nearest the outside of a turn.

Passive unweighting A reduction in pressure created as a result of skiing over convex terrain.

Passive weighting An increase in pressure due to terrain forces, created by skiing over concave terrain.

Pivoting Twisting skis about the axis of the legs.

Platform The moment in a turn when pressure is at a maximum, from which the skier initiates the following turn. Setting the edge creates a platform.

Pressure control Controlling pressure against skis using flexion and extension of legs.

Projection A twisting movement of the upper body or hips in the direction of the planned turn to create inertia, which is transferred to the skis in the turn.

Rebound The release of energy when pressure is removed from the ski. Similar to the effect of bouncing on a trampoline.

Rotation Twisting upper body in the same direction as skis are turning.

Sintered Ski base material which is cut from a solid block, not extruded and therefore harder, more porous and better able to absorb wax.

Skier's Code Basic rules of the road for skiers.

Snow guns/canons Machines which turn pressurized water into snow.

Snowcat A tracked vehicle used for snow grooming and transportation on snow.

Snowplough Skiing with skis in a 'V' shape, ski tips close together and tails pushed apart, resembling a plough or wedge. Skis ride on their inside edges.

Snowplough turn Changing direction while keeping skis in a plough position.

Stem Moving the tail of skis apart.

Stem turn A change in direction initiated by moving ski tails apart.

Telemark turn An old ski technique, requiring special equipment. The outside ski in the turn is forward of the inside ski and the heel of the rear foot is lifted from the ski.

Traversing Skiing across the fall line.

Unweighting A reduction of the pressure of the skis on the snow.

Up-unweighting Unweighting produced following an extension of legs. Unweighting takes place when the extension stops. The faster the extension, the more effective the movement is.

Up-weighting Increasing pressure on skis by extending legs. Pressure increases during extension; the faster the extension the more effective it is.

Visualization Creating a mental image of yourself successfully completing a manoeuvre.

Weighting Increasing pressure of skis against the snow.

X-country Cross-country skiing.

Bibliography

Bilodeau, Don, Andre Schwarz; *Skiing and Methodology*; Canadian Ski Instructor's Alliance, Montreal, 1981

Epp, Martin, Stephen Lee; *Avalanche Awareness*; The Wild Side, London, 1987

Killy, Jean Claude, with Doug Pfeiffer; *Skiing the Killy Way*; Simon and Schuster, New York, 1971

Parker, Paul; *Freeheel Skiing*; Chelsea Green Publishing Company, Chelsea, Vermont, 1988

Schweizerischer Interverband für Skiläufer: *Ski Suisse*; Habegger Verlag, Derendingen, 1985

Index